Frank Indiviglio, J.D., M.S.

Newts and Salamanders

Everything About Selection, Care,
Nutrition, Diseases, Breeding,
and Behavior

BARRON'S

CONTENTS

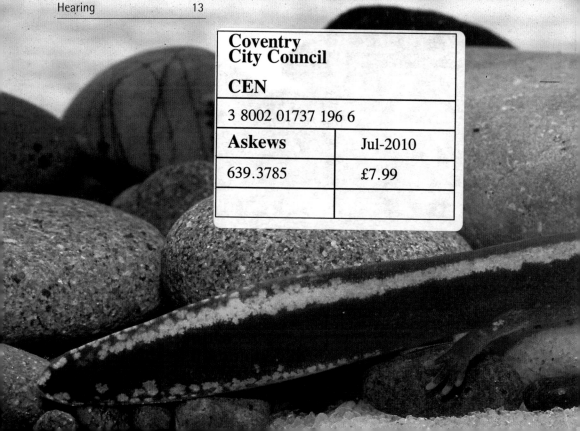

CLASSIFICATION AND CHARACTERISTICS OF SALAMANDERS

Salamanders, frogs, toads, and caecilians are amphibians, a group of animals that contains 6,433 species. This number changes over time as new species are discovered and, unfortunately, others become extinct.

The class Amphibia contains three orders:
1. Caudata, the newts and salamanders (580 species).
2. Anura, the frogs and toads (5,675 species).
3. Gymnophiona, the caecilians (174 species).

Lifestyles

Salamanders exhibit a surprising array of forms and lifestyles, and range in size from the .8-inch (20 mm) long Mexican lungless sala-mander, *Thorius arborius*, to the Japanese and Chinese giant salamanders, *Andrias japonicus* and *A. davidianus*, which approach 6 feet (180 cm) in length. There are eyeless salamanders

The 3.5-inch-long Northern two-lined salamander, Eurgcea bislineata, has neither lungs nor gills, and breathes entirely through its skin.

that dwell in caves, aquatic, arboreal, and two-legged species, and others that forgo metamor-phosis and breed as "adult larvae." Many guard their eggs, others give birth to fully developed young, and some walk across the snow to reproduce in frigid ponds.

Newt or Salamander?

The terms *newt* and *salamander* do not have a strict scientific definition, and are used inter-changeably for a number of species.

Newts

Most commonly, however, the term *newt* refers to small, semi-aquatic species within the family Salamandridae. Most exhibit sexual dimorphism, with males often changing color and developing crests during the breeding sea-son. Eggs are laid in water. Newt skin is often rough and brightly colored, without a significant mucous covering, and usually conceals glands housing a virulent poison, Tarichatoxin.

Salamanders

The term *salamander* is used for all other members of the order Caudata. Salamanders may be terrestrial, aquatic, or semi-aquatic; most lay eggs in water, but a few deposit them on land and at least three species bear live young.

The order Caudata is divided into nine to ten families (ten are listed here) and three suborders: the Cryptobranchoidea (giant and stream-dwelling Asian salamanders), the Salamandroidae (typical salamanders), and the Sirenoidea (the aquatic, two-legged sirens).

Suborder Cryptobranchoidea

Family Cryptobranchidae— the Giant Salamanders

This family contains the largest of all salamanders, the Chinese giant salamander, *Andrias davidianus,* which grows to lengths in excess of 5 feet (1.5 m). The Japanese giant salamander, *A. japonicus,* is nearly as large. The family's only other species, the hellbender, *Cryptobranchus alleganiensis,* resides in the northeastern and central United States. All three species inhabit clear, cool streams and are totally aquatic.

Giant salamanders undergo incomplete metamorphosis. Lungs develop but gill slits are retained, and eyelids do not form. Loose skin folds provide a large surface for oxygen absorption, but they can also breathe via the lungs.

These salamanders remain under other cover by day, and feed upon fish, snails, crayfish,

Contributions You Can Make

Only a very small number of fortunate people are paid to work with salamanders. Relevant education is a necessity, and volunteering at zoos or nature centers is an excellent way to gain practical experience.

Cooperation with zoos, museums, and other institutions will allow you to indulge your interests while helping to conserve salamanders. Possibilities include volunteering, participating in breeding programs, and assisting with state wildlife agency surveys.

worms, and other salamanders. The Chinese giant salamander may take ducks on occasion.

Giant salamanders and members of the family Hynobiidae are the only Caudates known to utilize external fertilization. Males hollow out a space beneath a rock and induce one or more females to lay eggs there. The male then releases sperm over the eggs and guards them for the two-to-three-month incubation period.

Family Hynobiidae— the Asiatic Salamanders

The 53 species in this family are largely confined to Asia; only one, the Siberian salamander, *Salamandrella keyserlingi,* extends into Eastern Europe. The hynobids are average-sized salamanders, the largest reaching 10 inches (25.4 cm) in length. The lungs are very small or absent, which seems to restrict them to living in or near cool streams, where oxygen levels are usually high. They tend to be terrestrial, but the eggs are laid in water.

As with the Cryptobranchidae, and in contrast to all other families, fertilization of the

Claws

Unique among the Caudates, salamanders of the genus *Hynobius* have claws, the function of which is as yet unknown.

eggs is external. The female lays two gelatinous packets, each of which contains up to 70 eggs. The male presses these egg capsules to his cloaca and releases sperm onto them. The males of several species have been observed to guard the eggs throughout incubation.

Suborder Salamandroidea

Family Salamandridae— the Brook Salamanders, Fire Salamanders, and Newts

This family, consisting of approximately 79 species, contains many animals that typically come to mind when most people hear the words *salamander* and *newt*. Representatives can be found in the United States, Europe, Asia, and northern Africa, a continent largely devoid of salamanders.

Those species that are termed *newts* generally spend about half of the year in water, but several have a larval aquatic stage, a land stage (during which they are termed *efts*), and finally a fully aquatic adult phase. Upon their return to water, the skin becomes thinner and smoother to facilitate oxygen transfer, and the tail and eyes change shape to aid swimming and allow for underwater vision. Lateral line organs, important for orientation and prey location, also develop, and the rear feet of some species become webbed.

The arboreal salamander, Bolitoglossa mexicanus, *frequently shelters within bromeliads.*

Caecilians are the least-studied of the amphibians.

The alpine salamander, *Salamandra atra*, gives birth to miniature versions of the adult stage as opposed to larvae. Several fire salamander (*Salamandra salamandra*) populations also use this method of reproduction, whereas others give birth to larvae.

Among this family there are several species that demonstrate an amazingly accurate ability to return to home ranges or breeding ponds, perhaps using polarized light, the earth's magnetic fields, or some as-yet-unknown mechanism. The red-bellied newt, *Taricha rivularis*, possesses extraordinary abilities in this regard. This resident of western North America has been observed to return to its breeding pond after being transported nine miles away. This feat is rendered all the more extraordinary by the fact that the tiny animals had to cross mountains and streams, some of which were the breeding habitats of other populations of the same species!

Family Amphiumidae— the Amphiumas or "Congo Eels"

This family contains three species of salamander in one genus, all of which live in the southeastern United States. The two-toed amphiuma, *Amphiuma means*, reaches a length of 46 inches (117 cm), and is the longest salamander in the Western Hemisphere.

The amphiumas have four tiny legs that are apparently useless for locomotion. The number of toes on the feet varies, and gives the three species their common names:

1. The one-toed amphiuma, *Amphiuma pholeter.*

2. The two-toed amphiuma, *Amphiuma means.*

3. The three-toed amphiuma, *A. tridactylum.*

Reproduction

Unique for a salamander, the male amphiuma transfers sperm directly into the female's cloaca. The larvae develop functional legs, but adults move by eel-like undulations of the body.

These three species are completely aquatic and retain certain larval characteristics, such as gill slits and lidless eyes.

Amphiumas may leave the water on rainy nights, with gravid females seeking shelter on damp land near water. The female coils around her 200 or so eggs for the entire incubation period of five months.

Family Proteidae— Mudpuppies and the Olm

The two genera in this family contain six species. Five are mudpuppies, genus *Necturus*, and the other genus contains only the olm, *Proteus anguinus*. The olm is a truly unusual creature, being found only in subterranean pools and streams in the western Balkan Peninsula and northern Italy. It is white and its tiny eyes are buried below the skin. Adults retain external gills and develop lungs.

Olms appear to use two breeding strategies. Sometimes eggs (15 to 65) are laid beneath a stone and guarded by both parents, and on other occasions the female gives birth to one or two well-developed larvae. The developing larvae are nourished by eggs that break down within the female's body.

The mudpuppies, or waterdogs, have external gills and lungs, and are found in eastern and central North America. Individuals from cool,

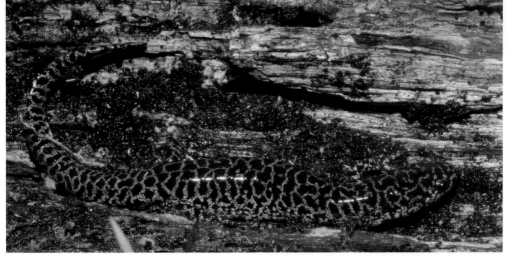

In common with most mole salamanders, the flatwoods salamander, **Ambystoma cingulatum,** *spends much of its life below ground.*

well-oxygenated waters have smaller gills than those from still, southern swamps. Mudpuppies are aquatic, and feed upon tadpoles, fishes, insects, snails, and crayfish. Males guard eggs during the one-to-two-month incubation period.

Family Ambystomatidae— the Mole Salamanders

The approximately 37 species in this family are generally stoutly built, burrowing creatures. Most have a dark brown or black background color, and are boldly patterned in contrasting stripes, spots, or blotches. The family is restricted to North America.

The common name, mole salamander, arises from the lifestyle of these salamanders. Adults lead a subterranean existence, emerging from their underground retreats only to breed or for short feeding forays.

Many mole salamanders breed in late winter or early spring. The spotted salamander, *Ambystoma maculatum*, has been observed

A rarely seen albino spotted salamander, **Ambystoma maculatum.**

crawling across snow to reach its breeding pond. The marbled salamander, *Ambystoma opacum*, lays eggs in dried pond beds in the fall. The female remains coiled around the eggs until rising water levels stimulate hatching.

Ambystomids always begin life as aquatic larvae and usually transform into terrestrial adults. Some populations of tiger salamanders, *Ambystoma tigrinum*, however, exhibit paedomorphism and sometimes reproduce without transforming into adult form. The Mexican axolotl, *Ambystoma mexicanum*, on the other hand, never transforms into a terrestrial adult. Tiger salamanders, *Ambystoma tigrinum*, may reach lengths in excess of

The voracious Pacific giant salamander, Dicamptodon ensatus, sometimes eats newborn mice, frogs, and other large prey items.

1 foot (30 cm), making them the largest of North America's terrestrial salamanders.

Family Dicamptodontidae— the Pacific Mole Salamanders

The three species in this family are sometimes classified within the family Ambystomatidae. The Pacific giant salamander, *Dicamptodon ensatus*, rivals the tiger salamander, *Ambystoma tigrinum*, in size, and resembles it in body form. These animals are found only in or near cool mountain streams along the northwestern coast of the United States. Cope's giant salamander, *Diacamptodon copei*, is neotenic, and never transforms into a terrestrial adult.

Interesting Fact
The family Plethodontidae is considered to be the most evolutionarily advanced.

In contrast to most other salamanders, the Pacific giant salamander makes noise when disturbed.

Family Rhyacotritonidae— the Torrent Salamanders

Believed to represent an early offshoot in the evolutionary history of the salamanders, the four torrent salamanders have vestigial lungs and are restricted in range to the extreme northwestern United States. They live only in the vicinity of cold, clear streams.

Family Plethodontidae— the Lungless Salamanders

The largest salamander family, Plethodontidae (the lungless salamanders), contains 391 species. Reaching its greatest diversity in the northeastern United States, the family contains a number of "typical woodland" species, including the red-backed salamander, *Plethodon cinereus,* and the slimy salamander, *P. glutinosus.*

Many unique adaptations and lifestyles are found in the family Plethodontidae. Perhaps the most unusual of all are to be found in the genus *Eurycea.* Typified by the eyeless, colorless Texas blind salamander, *Eurycea rathbuni,* most are neotenic and live out their lives in subterranean streams without ever seeing the light of day. Several new species have been recently described from the Edwards Aquifer in San Marcos, Texas. All are extremely limited in distribution and threatened by water pollution and habitat loss.

Members of the family Plethodontidae alone possess the nasolabial groove, a structure that, by capillary action, carries odors from the damp earth to the nose. All lack lungs and most are

Suborder Sirenoidea

Family Sirenidae—the Sirens

Sirens inhabit slow-moving bodies of water in the eastern and central United States and northeastern Mexico. They are completely aquatic, and have lungs and external gills, tiny front legs, and no rear legs. The body is long and eel-like. The greater siren, *Siren lacertina*, reaches a length of 37 inches (94 cm), and is thus one of the longest of all salamanders. The dwarf siren, *Pseudobranchus striatus*, is barely 10 inches (25 cm) long.

Their mode of fertilization is assumed to be external but is as yet unknown. Also unusual is the ability of some species to undergo aestivation. The thick mucous covering on the skin hardens and forms a type of cocoon around the animal, with an opening at the mouth. Sirens can wait out droughts of several months' duration in this state.

Uniqueness

The four species that make up the suborder Sirenoidea are so unique that some taxonomists have suggested creating a separate order for them.

without gills, breathing instead through the skin and lining of the mouth. As the skin must be moist for respiration to occur, they always live in damp places. The largest reaches about 8 inches (20 cm) and most are considerably smaller. Their small size allows for a greater surface area in proportion to volume, and thus increases respiratory efficiency.

Plethodontid lifestyles are a study in diversity. Some hatch from terrestrial eggs as mini-adults, whereas others are pale, gilled creatures with vestigial eyes that never leave underground streams. The grotto salamander, *Eurycea spelaeus*, migrates into subterranean cave pools upon metamorphosis, whereupon skin grows over its eyes, and the gills and skin pigment are lost.

The skin secretions of several lungless salamanders are quite sticky, and may function to gum up the jaws of snakes or other predators. Many appear to be territorial, marking and defending a specific home range. The porous, oxygen-permeable skins of the Plethodontids predispose them to pollution sensitivity, and many are becoming increasingly uncommon.

*The Texas blind salamander, **Eurycea rathbuni**, was first discovered in an artesian well nearly 200 feet below the ground, and occurs only in caves, wells, and pipes in San Marcos, Texas.*

CHARACTERISTICS OF SALAMANDERS

The range of adaptations that have evolved among salamanders rivals the diversity of their lifestyles and appearances.

Sight

The importance of sight varies among salamanders. Some, such as the lungless salamanders (family Plethodontidae), have binocular vision, whereas others, such as the olm, *Proteus anguinus*, function quite well without eyes. In contrast to other animals, the eyes are focused by moving the lens rather than by changing its shape. Some salamanders can distinguish eight different colors, and many can see their prey in near-total darkness.

Hearing

The available research seems to indicate that salamanders hear low-frequency sounds, and

Skin secretions of the Southeastern slimy salamander, Plethodon grobmani, *stick to the mouths of predators, thereby discouraging further aggression.*

that the inner ear is sensitive to ground-borne vibrations as well.

The Lateral Line

As an alternative way of "hearing," aquatic salamanders have a lateral line system by which they monitor water movement and detect other creatures. The lateral line is a series of pitlike depressions containing hair cells, or mechano-receptive neuromasts, and is located along the head and sides of the animal. It may also contain ampullary organs—electro-receptors that help the salamander orient itself, find prey, and escape predators.

Sense of Smell

Salamanders sense chemical aspects of their environment through two systems: the olfactory system (similar to the sense of smell in other animals), and the vomeronasal system.

The vomeronasal sense is used to sample chemical cues from substances in the mouth.

Lungless salamanders have a second way of using this sense. Small canals in each side of the snout (nasolabial grooves) draw fluids across the vomeronasal or Jacobson's organ. In this way, female red-backed salamanders, *Plethodon cinereus*, test the feces of males to determine the quality of their diet and their fitness as mates.

The Skin
Salamander skin is supplied with a variety of granular glands whose secretions are distasteful and potentially fatal if swallowed. Other skin

glands release mucus to prevent desiccation, assist in respiration, and repel harmful microorganisms.

In common with other amphibians, salamanders periodically shed their skin. The old skin splits around the mouth and is peeled back toward the tail and usually consumed.

Respiration
Depending upon the species, respiration is accomplished through the skin, gills, lungs, membranes of the mouth and throat, or a combination thereof. Those that breathe with lungs or throat membranes use throat pulsations (buccopharyngeal movements) to force air or water over or into these structures.

The lungless salamanders (Plethodontidae) breathe entirely through their skin (cutaneous respiration), but even salamanders equipped with gills and lungs use this method to some degree. Some aquatic species such as the hellbender, *Cryptobranchus alleganiensis*, have wrinkled skin folds that are moved about to increase their effective respiratory surface.

Reproduction
Salamanders use an incredible array of mating strategies. For the most part, breeding is seasonal in most temperate species, and is initiated by rainfall, an increase in day length or temperature, or a combination thereof. Tropical

Mexican axolotls, Ambystoma mexicanum, are neotenic and do not normally transform into terrestrial adults. This individual may have been chemically induced, or is possibly an axolotl/tiger salamander hybrid.

Adult grotto salamanders, Eurycea spelaea, *are blind, and have never been observed outside of caves.*

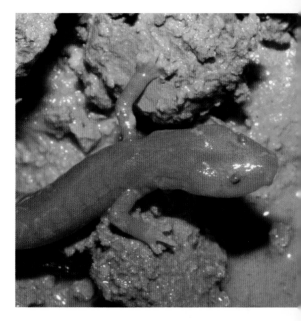

species may breed throughout the year or at the onset of the rainy season.

Males may attract females by releasing pheromones or, in some cases, by elaborate displays. Some male newts (i.e., *Triturus* spp.) develop enlarged dorsal fins to facilitate such displays. Eggs may be deposited and abandoned, guarded in water, or guarded on land.

Internal Fertilization

Fertilization is, with few exceptions, internal. The male deposits a sperm packet (spermatophore), which the female takes into her cloaca. The male may guide her to the spermatophore using an embrace (amplexus) or a form of controlled walking until she is directly over the sperm packet.

External Fertilization

Those salamanders that use external fertilization (Hynobiidae, Cryptobranchidae) reproduce

in water, with the male releasing sperm directly onto the eggs.

Larvae

Larvae hatching from aquatic eggs typically have external gills and, for a time, balancers, which are thin structures that prop the animal up from the mud at the pond's bottom, presumably to keep the gills clean. They are carnivorous, and, in contrast to tadpoles, the front limbs appear first.

Terrestrial eggs give rise to fully formed larvae. The fire salamander, *Salamandra salamandra*, gives birth to larvae with four legs and gills; the offspring in some populations are born as fully formed miniature adults.

The larvae of the marbled salamander, *Ambystoma opacum*, and the tiger salamander, *A. Tigrinum*, have been shown to select unrelated larvae as prey, and thus exhibit kin recognition.

Neoteny

Certain salamanders exhibit neoteny, a process wherein metamorphosis is not attained. Such animals, in effect, become sexually mature and breed while still larvae. Neoteny (or paedomorphosis) is usually associated with cold waters and may occur occasionally or always, depending on the species and the population.

Signs of Illness

A universal difficulty faced by those who care for animals is detecting sickness or injury in time for medical intervention to be effective.

It is always in a sick animal's best interests to appear healthy and alert, and to hide any symptoms of illness, so as to not draw the attention of predators. This instinctive behavior carries over into captivity.

Reproductive Pressures

The drive to reproduce also acts upon newts and salamanders in a way that complicates our ability to detect illness and disease. Females invariably allow only the fittest males to mate, and they are very good at rooting out "imposters." Female red-backed salamanders (*Pletho-don cinereus*), for example, examine dung piles left by males in order to assess their fitness. That evolution has fostered such a complicated behavior in so tiny a creature as a red-backed salamander, shows the importance of appearing healthy at all costs, and how carefully we must examine our salamander's appearances and behaviors.

Other Considerations

Unfortunately, amphibians, and in particular the more secretive salamanders, present especially challenging difficulties when it comes to assessing their health. While some newts prowl about during the day, seeking food (e.g., red-spotted newts, *Notopthalmus viridescens*), most salamanders are generally inactive, with hours spent in one position, often hidden, and food intake is fairly small. Therefore, signs of illness—indicated in other animals by activity levels, posture, and appetite—are minimal. Nevertheless, subtle clues can be detected with patient observation and experience.

Posture

With experience, one can often tell an ailing salamander by how it arranges itself at rest. Changes in limb, head position, and alertness are detectable once you know what to look for, but they are minute and virtually invisible to the untrained eye.

For example, while it is typical for a red salamander (*Pseudotriton ruber*) to lie with its body pressed to the ground and legs drawn in along its sides, the robust fire salamander (*Salamandra salamandra*) nearly always keeps its body elevated off the ground on sturdy limbs. A fire salamander that is splayed out on its stomach, in the manner of a red salamander, is likely ill.

The presence of this normally secretive red salamander, **Pseudotriton ruber,** *in an unsheltered area may indicate that it has been evicted from its burrows by a more aggressive tankmate.*

SALAMANDER BEHAVIOR

Location

Where in the terrarium or aquarium an individual positions itself is important, as many salamanders are quite regular in their choice of shelters or resting places. This is especially true for those, such as tiger salamanders (*Ambystoma tigrinum*), which are known to utilize the same burrows for years. If such a creature relinquishes its preferred shelter within the terrarium, a closer look is warranted. Competition from cage mates may be behind the behavior.

Be aware that aggressive behavior may take place after dark, or within caves and burrows. A nocturnal viewing bulb will assist you in observing your pets' nocturnal behavior.

A terrestrial animal that spends most of the time in its water dish is probably telling you that the terrarium is too dry, while a largely aquatic newt that refuses to enter the water may be signaling that an unacceptable rise in temperature has occurred.

Temperature

Movements may also be of diagnostic value— fossorial (burrowing), nocturnal species, such as marbled salamanders (*Ambystoma opacum*), for example, will come out in the day when heat stressed.

Overheating might also be signaled by an increase in the movements of the throat due to a faster breathing rate. Movement at odd times may also indicate that an individual is being harassed by a tankmate, or is not getting enough food.

Water Quality

Inappropriate pH levels or other chemical imbalances may cause agitated movements, especially in aquatic species. This may be accompanied by rubbing movements of the feet along the body.

Rapid throat pulsations may indicate that a salamander is experiencing heat stress.

Oxygen

Aquatic larvae, and adults of species that retain external gills (e.g., mudpuppies, *Necturus maculatus*), will wave the gills about in an effort to move water across them when dissolved oxygen levels fall. The hellbender (*Cryptobranchus alleganiensis*) engages in a unique rocking motion when its water is poorly oxygenated. By moving the loosely fitting skin about, they increase the skin's surface area that is in contact with the water, thereby assisting oxygen uptake. While the adults of the aforementioned species also have lungs and can rise to the surface for air, early stage larvae do not, and will perish if steps are not taken to oxygenate their water.

A drop in dissolved oxygen levels is usually indicative of another problem—a bacterial bloom, a temperature spike, or overcrowding, for example. Adding an air stone to the aquarium will address the symptoms, but not the problem.

Signs of Breeding Readiness

Restlessness may indicate that animals are in breeding condition, or that a female is gravid. This may be accompanied by a loss of appetite. There are sometimes physical changes in appearance, especially drastic in many male newts, which signal a readiness to breed.

HABITATS FOR CAPTIVE SALAMANDERS

Arranging proper living quarters for your collection is an important step in assuring good health, longevity, and breeding success. Well-planted terrariums are also beautiful to behold, and may well become household centerpieces.

Woodland Terrariums

Woodland terrariums for terrestrial salamanders are arranged to mimic conditions in a temperate forest: moderate temperatures, damp soil covered by dead leaves and moss, and shelters in the form of rocks, logs, and bark slabs. Shallow, easily exited water bowls should be provided as a safety measure. Rocks or cork bark placed in the bowl will prevent food insects from drowning.

Substrate

For a large, well-planted terrarium with few inhabitants, a semi-permanent situation may be created by using soil, coconut husk, and moss as a substrate. Be aware, however, that the soil must be changed from time to time,

With proper care, the brilliantly colored fire salamander, **Salamandra salamandra,** *may reach 50 years of age.*

and the more complex the terrarium, the harder this is to accomplish. If the tank is not crowded, it may be possible to remove and replace the top layers of earth without disturbing the overall setup.

An aesthetically pleasing and easily cleaned terrarium can be created without soil by arranging living or dried moss among rocks, weathered wood, and fallen leaves. In more elaborate, permanent setups, a layer of gravel should line the bottom of the tank to assist in drainage.

If soil is used, a little experimentation will help determine the proper consistency for burrowing animals; many will establish permanent retreats. Sphagnum moss mixed into the soil will improve moisture retention and prevent packing.

Humidity

Humidity is best controlled by using varying amounts of moisture-retaining materials, such as sphagnum moss, within the substrate and by providing shelters that retain dampness. The screen top should not be covered with plastic to increase humidity, as stagnant air has been implicated in health problems. Small misters are also available commercially.

Light

Lighting will generally be subdued, so live plants must be chosen accordingly. Peace lilies, pothos, cast iron plants, Chinese evergreens, and earth stars all do well in low-light situations.

Shoreline Terrariums

In the shoreline terrarium we will concentrate mainly on newts, which spend a good deal of time in the water but need a terrestrial resting place. Many attractive and interesting members of this family can be bred in captivity in a shoreline terrarium.

Land Areas

Because newts are generally well adapted to an aquatic existence, the water can be quite

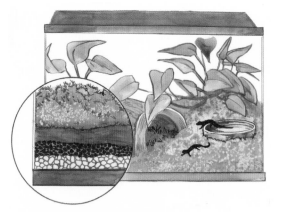

deep, provided that egress is simple. Floating cork bark or plants serve well as resting spots.

Ironwood and other sinking woods make excellent land areas. In a deepwater tank, they are especially useful in that newts can climb up the branching support areas on their way to the surface of the water.

Water Flow

It is important to assure that the outflow from your filter is mild. Most newts are not strong swimmers, and the constant stress of battling a strong current will weaken them and interfere with proper feeding. An undergravel or submersible filter, with the outflow directed upward, is ideal.

Gravel

Amphibian skin is delicate, so you must avoid using sharp or rough stones in their aquariums. Smooth, rounded gravel is acceptable, as long as the pieces cannot be swallowed by the aquarium's inhabitants.

Layers of moss, soil, charcoal, and gravel have been used to form the substrate.

Land areas can be fashioned from mounds of gravel. Plants (i.e., pothos) that thrive in wet gravel can be used to provide hiding places and also serve well as "ladders," enabling the newts to reach the surface of the water easily.

Gravel Cleaning

Even with effective filtration, gravel cleaning is a necessity. Siphon-based gravel washers are readily available and should be used each time a partial water change is provided.

Aquariums

Water Quality

Water quality is a paramount issue for all aquatic species, as they are confined to the same water into which they excrete their waste products, and their porous skin allows for easy infiltration of harmful chemicals.

Aquatic salamanders do little in the way of internal detoxification of their waste products. This functions well in the natural habitat, but can spell disaster in captivity. Effective filtration and partial or total water changes are therefore vital. See Filtration, page 25 for further details.

As a general rule, provide aquatic salamanders with the largest volume of water possible. Powerful filters can be used with larger species, especially if a sheltered retreat is provided.

Preventing Escapes

Newts exhibit a remarkable ability to crawl up glass, so a secure cover is a must. Escapees usually desiccate before being recovered.

===== TIP =====

Observing Secretive Species

Salamanders can often be habituated to using a shelter that is alongside the terrarium's glass, to allow for easier viewing. For particularly shy animals, black paper can be taped to the glass and lifted for viewing, or it can be removed for gradually increasing times each day until the salamander remains in the shelter without it.

In general, hellbenders, amphiumas, sirens, mudpuppies, and other large aquatic salamanders are best kept in bare-bottom aquariums equipped with powerful filters. Frequent partial or total water changes are a must.

Trout Holding Tanks

Trout holding tanks provide ideal environments for large salamanders. They are equipped with chillers and powerful filters, so even the most demanding cold-water species can be accommodated.

Salamander Larvae

Keeping salamander larvae in an aquarium poses a unique set of problems. Although a large water volume is generally desirable (to promote growth and dilute waste products), larvae need to eat a great deal, and fare best when literally surrounded by food. Patient observation will reveal the right balance between space and food availability.

The larvae must be able to avoid each other, as all are cannibalistic. Filling the tank with

Salamander larvae are cannibalistic. Here a young Mexican axolotl, **Ambystoma mexicanum,** *consumes a tank-mate.*

artificial or real plants, especially those with lots of feathery branches, will help somewhat.

Water flow is critical. Most larvae are weak swimmers and are easily sucked into filter intakes. Undergravel, sponge, and corner filters are the safest choices.

TIP

Excessive Humidity

There is some evidence that a very wet environment will cause arboreal salamanders (*Bolitoglossa* spp.) to shed their tails and expire, apparently because of excessive water uptake. Try providing a moist retreat but fairly low ambient humidity.

Young salamanders eat constantly, and water changes are the surest way of avoiding losses caused by ammonia toxicity. Waste product buildup will lead to abnormally slow growth, sickness, or even death.

Tropical Forest Terrariums

Whereas frogs and caecilians exhibit their greatest diversity in tropical forests, salamanders are poorly represented. Available rain-forest species are often terrestrial and arboreal. Daily spraying and a small pool are beneficial in maintaining the high humidity that they require. These methods are preferable to using a glass cover to raise humidity, as fresh air is also necessary.

Arboreal salamanders should also be provided with moss-filled arboreal caves, and live plants containing a small pool of water at their base.

Outdoor Terrariums

Large outdoor terrariums have great potential, especially in the area of captive breeding, as exposure to a natural seasonal cycle is critical to reproductive success with many salamanders. A shaded location is best, although morning sun exposure is beneficial as long as the inhabitants are able to remain cool and moist by burrowing beneath leaves, logs, or soil.

Behavioral Observations

The range of behaviors that you can observe in an outdoor enclosure will far exceed those available in a limited indoor situation. To enhance the experience, consider using night-vision glasses or commercially available night-viewing bulbs.

Wood, dead leaves, and ripe fruit will attract isopods, millipedes, and insects. You may find that you'll need to provide little if any additional food. Outdoor enclosures for large aquatic salamanders offer limitless possibilities—even swimming pools can be used.

The Terrarium's Physical Parameters

Where captive amphibians are concerned, proper environmental conditions are, in a sense, preventive medicine. We know very little about the nature and treatment of the diseases that afflict salamanders. Providing them with optimal living conditions is essential in reducing stress that weakens the immune system and is at the root of many illnesses.

The ringed salamander, **Ambystoma annulatum,** *appears aboveground only after dark.*

pH Levels

pH indicates water's acidity or alkalinity. The pH scale runs from 0 to 14, with 7 being neutral, 1 being highly acidic, and 14 being highly alkaline. Most salamanders do well at a pH of 6.5 to 7.5. Soil pH also affects terrestrial salamanders, and many have been disappearing from habitats where acid rain has lowered the pH. Cave-dwelling salamanders or those that live in creeks running over limestone will likely be adapted to a very alkaline environment.

There are a variety of commercially available test kits and strips that are simple to operate and that instantly measure pH levels. The pH of water changes over time. Waste products, uneaten food, and decaying plants in the aquarium will all lead to an acidic condition. Most amphibians are stressed at levels below 6, and many die at a pH of 5.5 or below.

Signs of pH Stress

Animals suffering pH stress will at first appear restless and may move at times when they are not usually active. They will then

Acid Exposure

Salamanders suffering from exposure to acidic conditions can be revived by a soaking in cool, clean water. For terrestrial or debilitated aquatic species, keep the water low enough so that the salamander can breathe without having to swim to the surface.

become lethargic and appear to lack muscle tone when picked up.

Making pH Changes

In general, the rule is to make pH changes slowly. Rapid pH changes of two points or more kill most fishes and may be fatal to salamanders as well.

Ammonia

Ammonia is a poisonous intermediate by-product of the breakdown of organic material by bacteria and is also excreted by salamanders along with their waste products. Salamanders are extremely sensitive to ammonia levels, both in the water and on land. Because ammonia is colorless and odorless and *extremely* lethal, it presents a particularly difficult problem in the captive maintenance of amphibians. An ammonia test kit, available at pet stores, is an invaluable amphibian keeper's tool.

Removing Ammonia

Water or substrate changes are indispensable in removing ammonia from an aquarium or terrarium. The nitrifying bacteria living on well-established filter media and the gravel over undergravel filter plates also do an excellent job of detoxifying ammonia. Ammonia-removing media can be placed into filter boxes; follow the manufacturer's instructions regarding the amount to use.

Copper

Copper is an ingredient in some amphibian medications, but at high levels it is toxic. Copper pipes, most common in older buildings, will leach copper at varying levels throughout the day. In the morning, if the water has not been used all night, copper levels will be very high. Copper content may be negligible after several hours of use. A test kit should be used to check your water supply at various times during the day to determine if and when copper is present.

Chlorine, Chloramine, and Other Additives

Chlorine and chloramine must be removed from water used in salamander enclosures. Liquid preparations, which work instantly, are available at most pet stores. Chlorine, but not chloramine, can also be removed by allowing water to stand in an open container for 24 hours. Aeration will speed the process somewhat.

Humidity

Generally, salamanders require high humidity and small microhabitats within the terrarium where it is very damp. A pool, especially if it is in contact with the substrate, will go a long way in raising humidity levels. Frequent spraying of the terrarium may be necessary for terrestrial species that are reluctant to use a water bowl. Be sure to remove chlorine and chloramine from water used to spray the terrarium.

Fast-moving streams and rivers in Eastern Texas and Western/Central Louisiana are the only known habitat of the Gulf Coast waterdog, **Necturus bayeri.**

Filtration

The Undergravel Filter

Undergravel filters effectively transform the entire aquarium substrate into a biological filter. Water drawn through the gravel and returned to the surface via plastic tubes nourishes beneficial aerobic bacteria and inhibits the growth of harmful anaerobic bacteria.

The return tubes can be cut so that even a small pool in a terrarium or a very shallow aquarium can be filtered. A power-head can be added directly to the return tube to increase the flow of water through the system. Undergravel filters are especially useful when rearing larvae and small salamanders because they cannot injure animals with suction and strong currents.

Gravel Washers

A gravel washer is a siphon tube used to remove particulate matter that is trapped in the gravel bed (uneaten food and feces are not removed by an undergravel filter but rather

TIP

Encouraging Aerobic Bacteria

When replacing filter media (e.g., carbon, floss, filter pads), always retain a bit of the old material and add it to the new batch. This will introduce beneficial aerobic bacteria, which will quickly repopulate the new filter.

are drawn into the gravel bed). The particulate material may be rendered chemically harmless through the action of aerobic bacteria, but it will still cloud the water if not removed. Reverse flow undergravel filters help to alleviate this problem.

A mechanical filter may be used in addition to an undergravel filter.

When using an undergravel filter, make sure that the gravel used is too large to be be swallowed by your salamanders as they feed.

Regular Water Changes

The use of a filter does not eliminate the need for regular water changes. Even in a highly efficient system with both undergravel and mechanical filtration, ammonia will build up and must be physically removed periodically. Depending on the population of salamanders and the size of the aquarium, a 20–30 percent weekly water change is usually essential.

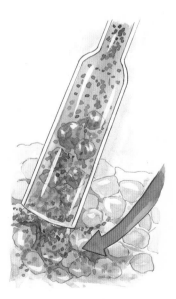

TIP

Instant Water Clarifiers

Avoid products that claim to "instantly clarify water." If the water in your tank is cloudy, there is a reason, and masking that condition without correcting it will lead to the death of your specimens. Water clarity is not necessarily an indication that the water is chemically safe. Ammonia is virtually colorless and odorless except at high concentrations.

A simple aquarium ammonia test kit will assist in determining the ideal timing and volume of water changes required for your aquarium. Periodic changes will also prevent pH drift, yellowing of the water, and other undesirable conditions.

Corner Filters

Operated by external air pumps, these "old-fashioned" inside-the-tank filters are actually quite effective if the airflow to them is sufficiently powerful. In addition to providing mechanical filtration, bacteria growing on the filter medium will assist in ammonia detoxification.

Ideally, a corner filter should have low and high intake holes, so that water will be pulled from the very bottom of the tank and at a slightly higher level. As with the undergravel filter, the outflow of water is directed upward so that strong currents that might disturb larvae are not established.

A gravel washer will remove debris that becomes lodged in the gravel bed.

A tiny range—three mountainsides in Arkanasas—leaves the Fourche Mountain salamander,
Plethodon fourchensis, vulnerable to extinction. Little is known of its natural history.

Biological Filtration

Biological filtration is the most important of the three basic filtration processes. Suspended solids and chemicals are removed from the aquarium through mechanical and chemical filtration respectively.

In biological filtration, aerobic bacteria (microorganisms that require the presence of oxygen) convert ammonia, which is highly toxic, to less harmful compounds known as nitrites and nitrates. Ammonia and other nitrogenous compounds enter the aquarium through dead animals and plants, uneaten food, and feces. The organisms involved in the process, *Nitrosomas* and *Nitrobacter* bacteria, live and reproduce on substrates that are continually bathed with oxygenated water (i.e., gravel, filter pads, carbon, and "bio-balls").

Aerobic bacteria starter cultures may be purchased or obtained from the gravel in a well-established tank.

Sponge Filters

Sponge filters provide mechanical and biological filtration, and are ideal for use with larvae and delicate specimens. The filter should be
periodically cleaned by rinsing it in cool water
(hot water will kill the beneficial bacteria on
the sponge). Chemical filtration is not provided,
so regular water changes are particularly
important.

Other Inside Filters

Inside filters combining a motor and a filtration unit within a single submersible container
are also available. These can be operated in
fairly low water and are available in a variety of
sizes, including tiny models suitable for goldfish
bowls. They vary greatly in effectiveness, but
many provide effective mechanical and biological filtration and varying degrees of chemical
filtration.

Hanging Outside Filters

These filters hang outside the aquarium and
have tubes that extend into the water, and are
ideal for use with mudpuppies, sirens, axolotls,
and other aquatic salamanders. Some models
will not operate unless the aquarium is nearly
filled with water, whereas others operate well
in partially filled aquariums.

The siphon tubes should be secured with duct
tape so that they cannot be dislodged by large
salamanders. To create an escape-proof environment, be sure to carefully tape over the
point where the tubes enter the aquarium.

Canister Filters

Canister filters rest on the floor below the
aquarium. The tubes entering the aquarium
are flexible and can be fitted into small holes

TIP

Rocks in the Aquarium

Water chemistry can be affected by rocks
that are introduced into the aquarium.
Always choose tried and proven aquarium
trade staples such as shale and schist.

cut into the tank top, rendering them difficult
to dislodge. Canister filter motors are usually
more powerful than those supplied with other
filters, and so are well suited for use with large
specimens.

Commercial Preparations

A variety of preparations are available for
altering water chemistry. Among the most useful are those that instantly remove chlorine and
chloramine from tap water.

There are also liquids that help replace the
mucous coat (marketed for fish, but safe for
use with salamanders), leach heavy metals from
the water, and set the pH to a specific level.

Lighting

UVB Light

It is now well established that many reptiles
require light within a certain wavelength (Ultraviolet B) in order to synthesize vitamin D and
thereby utilize dietary calcium. The same has not
been shown to hold true for most amphibians.
In fact, the increased ultraviolet light that is
currently reaching the earth (perhaps because

of a thinning of the ozone layer) has been linked to amphibian population declines.

Salamander eggs that are deposited in open water and exposed to sunlight are protected by ultraviolet-blocking compounds. It may therefore follow that at least certain concentrations of ultraviolet light are harmful to amphibian eggs and, possibly, the larvae. Most salamanders do not, in the natural state, experience long-term exposure to ultraviolet light, and it seems unnecessary to provide such in captivity.

UVA Light

Ultraviolet A light waves have been shown to function in the regulation of circadian rhythms and in promoting natural behaviors, including reproduction, in a variety of animal species. A variety of fluorescent lights, emitting UVA and little or no UVB, are now available for use with amphibians.

Fluorescent bulbs give off little heat. Except in tiny or poorly ventilated terrariums, temperature should be largely unaffected. Incandescent bulbs should be avoided because of the large amount of heat generated, although a very small bulb might be used to create a day/night cycle.

"Night-Viewing" Lights

Red and black tinted bulbs designed to allow for the observation of nocturnal pets are a great boon to salamander enthusiasts. As of this writing, available models are incandescent; therefore, heat buildup must be monitored. Fluorescent models might allow for a complete switching of the day/night cycle, just as is done in the nocturnal houses of many zoos.

An unusually large, stout black-bellied sala-mander, **Desmognathus quadrimaculatus.**

Inducing Breeding

The breeding cycle of most salamanders is strongly tied to seasonal climatic changes. Captives may live for decades but fail to reproduce unless temperature, humidity, water level, and other such factors are varied appropriately.

Rain Chambers

Artificial rain chambers have been successfully used to induce breeding in a great many frog species, and are well worth trying with terrestrial salamanders. Small models are available commercially, or can be set up with a submersible pump or canister filter. In either case, the filter's return tubes are fastened to the terrarium's screen top and used to distribute water in a pool as "rain." The optimal timing and length of the rains are best determined by researching your pet's natural habitat, and can be controlled by an electric timer.

Light Cycles

Although most salamanders are nocturnal, it is important to stimulate a normal seasonal light cycle. This can be easily done with a timer,

A splendid male banded newt, **Ommatotriton vittatus,** *in breeding condition.*

matching the day/night cycle to that which occurs in your salamander's natural habitat.

If you live within the natural range of the salamanders that you keep, you can also set the terrarium in a location where it will experience a natural light cycle, i.e., near, but not directly in front of, an unshaded window.

Artificial Ponds

Many terrestrial salamanders need access to a body of water in which to lay their eggs, along with rising temperatures and a "rainy season." Because the size of the pond may affect their reproductive output, you'll want to provide the largest container possible and be sure that the animals can easily exit the water area (most swim poorly and can easily drown).

For certain semi-aquatic salamanders, a mere increase in water volume may be enough to stimulate reproduction. For example, crested newts (*Triturus cristatus*) moved from a 15-gallon (57 L) to a 55-gallon (208 L) aquarium may come into breeding condition despite not having been subjected to a cooling-off period.

Manipulating Temperature

Most temperate salamanders need exposure to a period of reduced temperatures if they are to reproduce. The artificial winter need not be as long as a true winter (four to six weeks is often sufficient), and temperatures usually need not be dropped as low as would occur in the natural situation.

Warnings: Electrical Hazards

- Pumps, filters, chillers, lights, and such cannot be indiscriminately added to one's circuitry; consult an electrician.
- All warnings on each appliance must be adhered to.
- Do not add extension cords randomly as your collection grows. Note the rating of each cord and of the equipment you plug into it.
- Free-roaming or escaped pets can upset lights and heaters and cause fires.
- Be especially careful of portable room heaters; not all are designed to operate continuously.
- Be certain that incandescent bulbs are not close to flammable objects or plants, and that they are housed in fixtures that are appropriate in terms of wattage used and length of time operated.

A refrigerator, unheated basement, or attic can be used, and there has been some success in the overwintering of certain species outdoors. When using these options, be sure to take the temperatures at different times of the year to establish an overall pattern beforehand.

Cleaning

Bleach

Logs, rocks, and other objects to be added to the enclosure should be carefully examined for potentially harmful invertebrates and decomposing organic matter. They should then be soaked overnight in a solution of 1/2 cup of household (5 percent) bleach per gallon of water, followed by a thorough rinsing. As wood, porous rock, and similar materials may retain bleach within their structures, they should also be immersed in water to which a commercial instant dechlorinating agent (available at any aquarium store) has been added.

"Old-Fashioned" Techniques

Salt, although not much in favor today, is a very effective cleaning aid, as is plain hot water—both have long been used with great success in public and private collections. Allowing enclosures, rocks, and other items, to dry in the sun is an often overlooked but very effective aspect of terrarium cleaning and disinfection.

Methylene Blue

This tropical fish medication can be used for soaking aquariums that have housed sick animals and as a medicine in certain circumstances. A drawback is that it stains certain types of wood, and will temporarily discolor human and amphibian skin.

Terrarium Substrates

Moss and soil must also be cleaned or replaced at regular intervals, as ammonia will build up within these as it does in water. If lightly used, carpet and sphagnum moss can be rinsed once or twice before being discarded.

Commercial Disinfectants

Novolsan, Microquat, and similar disinfectants are widely used in zoos but are not recommended for amphibians except in very limited disease-control situations. Several less-powerful products, marketed as being safe for amphibians, are available in the pet trade.

NUTRITION AND FEEDING TECHNIQUES

Nutrition is a topic of extreme importance and complexity, and a discussion of it touches upon nearly every other topic addressed in this book. Captive reproduction is particularly dependent on proper nutrition, and success in this area may necessitate short-term changes in the type and amount of food offered.

The type of diet to be fed depends on many factors, including your salamanders' ages, the temperature at which they are maintained, and the nature of their tank-mates.

Food

The type of terrarium in which the salamanders live will affect the way in which food is presented. Factors such as whether an uneaten food animal will live or die in the tank and how one will keep track of the food eaten by secretive terrarium inhabitants must all be considered.

House Crickets (*Acheta domestica*)

The commercially available house cricket can be an important food source for some

This Chinese fire-bellied newt, Cynops orientalis, *is in good weight . . . fed well but not obese.*

salamander species, but softer-bodied prey (e.g., blackworms or earthworms) are generally preferable as dietary staples. Pinhead and ten-day-old crickets may be one of the few practical foods to use when rearing small terrestrial species such as the red-backed salamander (*Plethodon cinereus*).

Crickets are drawn to water bowls and will drown quickly if not provided with a means of easy egress (e.g., cork bark or plastic plants in the bowl). Small individuals may escape through the terrarium's screen top, and uneaten crickets will quickly lose any vitamin/mineral powder with which they have been coated.

How Many to Feed: It is generally preferable to feed several small crickets as opposed

Warning

Crickets have distinctly carnivorous leanings and may attack lethargic or injured salamanders.

The wide mouth of the 12-inch-long barred tiger salamander, Ambystoma mavortium mavortium, *allows it to feed upon other salamanders and even small rodents.*

to one large one. Small crickets present more surface area to the action of digestive enzymes, and contain a proportionately lower volume of indigestible body parts such as legs and wings.

Red and Confused Flour Beetle Larvae, *Tribolium castaneum* and *T. confusum*

The larvae, or grubs, of tiny flour beetles are readily accepted by many tiny amphibians, and are an important source of dietary variety for small terrestrial salamanders.

Colonies are available commercially, or the beetles may be collected from old boxes of dog biscuits. The biscuits provide all the food, moisture, and shelter that the colony needs.

Using Flour Beetles: Tap a grub-laden biscuit over a petri dish and place the dish in the terrarium. If introduced directly onto the substrate, the grubs will burrow rapidly and render it diffi-

cult to determine if they are being eaten. Some salamanders accept the adult beetles as well.

Springtails (*Collembolla* sp.)

Springtails are tiny, primitive insects that can be collected from beneath damp leaf litter. They are also available commercially, and feed readily upon decaying vegetation and tropical fish food flakes. Because of their size, springtails are suitable for only the smallest salamanders and their larvae, but are important in that food options for such species are limited.

Mealworms (*Tenebrio molitor, Zophobus morio*)

Mealworms, two species of which are commonly available, are the larvae of darkling and related beetles. It is best to use only newly molted (white in color) individuals as salamander food, as they possess strong mouthparts and may cause injuries to salamanders. Diets rich in mealworms have also been linked to intestinal blockages in a number of amphibian species.

Care: Mealworms will shed most frequently when fed heavily and kept at 76–80°F (24–27°C). They should be housed in a mix of wheat bran, powdered baby food, and a bit of tropical fish food flakes, with banana skins as a moisture source.

Pupae: Mealworm pupae are a fine newt food, and are taken by some terrestrial salamanders as well. They likely have a different nutrient profile than either the larvae or adults.

Mealworm Beetles: Beetles make up the world's largest animal family, and figure prominently in the diets of wild newts and salamanders. Newly transformed beetles are soft and brown in color, and are preferable to larvae and older beetles as a food item.

Earthworms (*Lumbricus terrestris* and related species)

The earthworm can be used as the major portion of the diet, up to 75 percent or so, of a wide variety of aquatic and terrestrial salamanders.

Some Cautions: Earthworms consume dirt while foraging, and concentrate insecticides or pollutants that are in their habitat. Thus far, this has proven of concern only around golf

Earthworm-Only Diets

In experimental situations, newly transformed spotted salamanders (*Ambystoma maculatum*) and northern red salamanders (*Pseudotriton ruber*) fed solely upon earthworms grew rapidly and matured into healthy, vigorous adults.

courses (because of unusually high pesticide usage). Commercial worm farms sometimes feed their stock with manure from local chicken farms. It is not known if this practice presents a *Salmonella*-transmission concern.

Size of Food Items: It is preferable to feed a small entire earthworm, but cut pieces can be used (these will decompose if uneaten). In damp sphagnum moss, uneaten earthworms will generally live until captured, but may burrow out of reach in soil. Earthworms can survive in cool, aerated water for eight hours or so.

Breeding Earthworms: Earthworms do best at temperatures below 70–75°F (21–24°C), and can be kept in a plastic container with alternating layers of dead leaves and topsoil that are kept moist but not wet. Ventilation is crucial, but the top must also be secure, as earthworms "wander" at night.

Earthworms should be provided a varied diet of dead leaves, bread crumbs, cornmeal, fish-food flakes, and overripe vegetables. Damp burlap laid on the surface will cause earthworms to congregate below, allowing for easy collection. Having a breeding colony assures a constant supply of tiny worms, which provide a more nutritious diet for small animals than do pieces of large worms.

Waxworms (*Galleria mellonella*)

Waxworms are caterpillars that live in beehives. They are shipped packed in sawdust, and any that adheres to their bodies must be removed before they are used as salamander food. They should be refrigerated until needed.

Waxworms are higher in fat (58 percent) than are most other insects, but are safe to use as approximately 20 percent of the diet of most salamanders. Choose smaller over larger waxworms, as the exoskeleton is quite thick and may present a digestive hazard.

Fruit Flies (*Drosophila melanogaster* and related species)

Fruit flies are useful for the tiny species and newly transformed salamanders. Cultures of various species, including flightless strains, are widely available.

Houseflies (Family Muscidae) and Phoenix Worms (*Hermetia illucens*)

Fly cultures, including flightless strains, are commercially available. Both the larvae (maggots) and adults are readily accepted by most salamanders.

Phoenix worms are the larvae of black soldier flies, and may also be purchased from insect suppliers. Reaching ¾ of an inch (2 cm) in length, they are hardy soft-bodied, and said to contain an ideal calcium:phosphorus profile.

TIP

Pesticide Concerns

Do not collect insects from areas where pesticides are used regularly, or for approximately one week after your collection site has been treated as part of a West Nile virus or similar control program. Your local mosquito-control authority can supply you with a treatment schedule.

Wild-Caught Invertebrates

Wild-caught invertebrates impart much-needed variety to captive diets, and should, where possible, form a significant portion of the food offered to your collection.

Field Plankton: Swinging through tall grass with a net will yield a variety of useful (and interesting!) invertebrates, collectively termed *field plankton*. To feed small salamanders, empty the net's contents into a container with holes that will allow only the tiniest insects to exit.

Collecting Other Invertebrates: Commercial or homemade light traps, or even a nightly check of a porch light, can supply your pets with nutritious food items throughout the warmer months. Slugs and small snails are eagerly taken by many salamanders, and aphids can be an important source of dietary variety for small, terrestrial species. Boards placed on the ground will attract a variety of invertebrates, which can be harvested as needed.

*This greater siren, *Siren lacertina*, is, in contrast to most individuals, brilliantly marked with gold spots.*

Commercially Available "Wild" Invertebrates

Grasshoppers, silkworms, tomato hornworms, sow bugs, and other invertebrates are bred commercially and should be used on a regular basis.

Canned Invertebrates: Canned invertebrates represent an important new food source for captive amphibians. Particularly useful are those species that are difficult to otherwise gather in large numbers, such as snails, grasshoppers, mole crickets, and silkworms. Most are readily accepted by newts and aquatic salamanders. Terrestrial salamanders generally take live food only, but many can be easily trained to feed from tongs. (Be sure to use plastic tongs, as metal can cause mouth injuries.)

Other Food Sources

Brine Shrimp: These shrimplike creatures are one of the few tiny live food items that are

commercially available. Adults, eggs, and hatchery kits are sold at most pet stores. Brine shrimp should be allowed to feed on commercially available nutrient-loading diets for a day or two before being offered to your pets, and must be rinsed to remove salt traces.

Daphnia: Daphnia are easily collected and cultured in pond water, and feed upon algae, decaying grass, and algae tablets (tropical fish food). Because of their small size, daphnia are suitable for only the tiniest of larvae.

Mosquito Larvae: These all-too-abundant insects can be collected with a finely meshed dip net from stagnant pools of water. Be aware that mosquito larvae transform into adults rapidly, so feed only as many as will be consumed immediately.

Blackworms (*Lumbriculus variegatus*)

These earthworm relatives have been used successfully as the sole diet for Mexican axolotl (*Ambystoma mexicanum*) and other species, and are among the most useful of all larval foods.

Blackworms will live for at least two weeks in the refrigerator if their water is changed daily (dead worms float when the water is disturbed and should be discarded). Uneaten blackworms will live in an aquarium, and are actually quite effective scavengers. They also thrive in damp sphagnum moss, and can therefore be fed to terrestrial salamanders as well.

Blackworms, even those that have been chopped to size for small larvae, clump together once introduced to an aquarium, and may present a choking hazard. The use of a commercial worm feeder will limit this, especially if it is positioned near a filter's outflow.

Blackworms should not be confused with tubifex worms, which are harvested from

---

═══════ T I P ═══════

Invertebrate Traps

There are a number of ways to collect invertebrates. A jar buried flush with the ground (cover with a board propped up by a stone) and baited with beer-soaked paper (for snails and slugs) or fruit will yield a surprising array of creatures. Termites will flock to a PVC pipe baited with damp cardboard and situated near a colony. By placing a sheet below a bush and beating the foliage, you can collect large quantities of caterpillars, spiders, katydids, beetles, and other invertebrates.

The Pigeon Mountain salamander, Plethodon petraeus, *is known only from the eastern slope of the Pigeon Mountain in Northwestern Georgia.*

polluted waters. Tubifex worms have been implicated in amphibian gastrointestinal diseases and human skin rashes.

Crayfish

Hellbenders, sirens, amphiumas, and mudpuppies feed heavily upon crayfish in the wild, and newts readily accept small bits of crayfish meat. Crayfish contain high concentrations of vitamin E, and store well under refrigeration. Unless the crayfish is soft (recently molted), its claws should be removed.

Fish

Whole fish are an excellent food for aquatic salamanders. Their calcium:phosphorus ratio is approximately 2:1, and therefore ideal. Pond-raised minnows and shiners are the most nutritious choices, but guppies, platys, mollies, and goldfishes (see box, "Goldfish") should also be offered.

Wild fishes can be collected via seine net or minnow trap (check local regulations before collecting).

Amphibians

Amphibian eggs and larvae are likely important prey items for wild salamanders, but I do not advocate collecting them as food. However, a breeding pair of Mexican axolotls, *Ambystoma mexicanum*, can produce hundreds of easily hatched eggs with which to feed your collection.

The use of adult salamanders as food is largely precluded, because of the presence of skin toxins in most. Marine toads have expired instantly upon consuming tiny red spotted newts, *Notopthalmus viridescens*.

Rodents

Rodent-based diets have been linked to corneal opacities and kidney and liver problems

Goldfish

Goldfish-only diets have been implicated in fatalities among aquatic turtles, but the reasons behind this phenomenon are as yet unclear. They can, however, be safely used on an occasional basis for captive salamanders.

in insectivorous amphibians and reptiles. Pacific giant salamanders, *Dicamptodon ensatus*, tiger salamanders, *Ambystoma tigrinum,* and other large species no doubt take nestling rodents on occasion, but field research has revealed that invertebrates form the overwhelming bulk of their diets. Rodents are not recommended as food for captive salamanders.

Commercially Prepared Foods

Trout chow and Reptomin Floating Food Sticks have great potential as a staple diet for those salamanders that will accept nonliving prey, and can constitute up to 85 percent of the diet of Mexican axolotls, *Ambystoma mexicanum.*

Freeze-dried, frozen, and canned invertebrates, marketed for tropical fish and reptiles, offer an excellent means of providing salamanders with valuable dietary variety. Newts, sirens, amphiumas, and other aquatic species hunt largely by scent, and readily accept such pet trade staples as *Gammarus*, prawns, bloodworms, beef heart, *Cyclops,* and mosquito larvae. Invertebrates not readily available to most hobbyists, such as grasshoppers, mole crickets, snails, and silkworms, are now available in cans and can be tong-fed to a wide variety of salamanders.

Vitamin and Mineral Supplementation

Dietary supplementation for captive salamanders is a poorly studied topic. Perhaps the greatest stumbling block in deciding which, if any, supplements to use is the fact that we do not know what constitutes a balanced diet for most species.

A wide variety of vitamin/mineral supplements are marketed for captive amphibians. As a general guideline, animals maintained on

TIP

Timing Meals

Crickets and other invertebrates quickly lose their vitamin/mineral coating when wandering about in a terrarium. To avoid this, provide food at a time when the salamanders are likely to feed immediately, feed by forceps, or confine food to a dish.

fewer food items, and young salamanders, will likely need a greater degree of supplementation than those fed a varied diet containing wild-caught invertebrates.

For example, a three-toed amphiuma, *Amphiuma means*, consuming a diet consisting of minnows, crayfish, earthworms, blackworms, waxworms, crickets, and snails, would likely need no supplementation. However, red-backed salamanders, *Plethonodon cinereus*, provided with only ten-day-old crickets, might need to have supplementation with most of their meals.

Food Animals' Diet

To increase their nutritional value, food animals should themselves consume a nutritious diet before being offered to your collection. Tropical-fish flakes are readily consumed by crickets and earthworms, as is trout chow. This is a good way of providing some of the benefits of such prepared diets to salamanders that will consume only living prey. Oranges, green vegetables, yams, and similar foods will also improve the nutritional profile of crickets, roaches, and other invertebrates.

HEALTH

When considering salamander health care, it is important to bear in mind that amphibian skin is extremely porous. This fact will affect the medication that can be used.

Products designed for tropical fishes play an important role in amphibian medicine, but one should begin treatment with a concentration that is only 50 percent of that recommended for fish because salamanders have a greater surface area for the absorption of medications than do most fishes.

Here is other helpful advice.

• A relationship with a veterinarian well versed in amphibian medicine is an absolute necessity.

• Basic hygiene is the starting point for avoiding illnesses and, in some cases, for treatment.

• Bottled spring (not distilled) water should always be on hand for an emergency, as when you may need to flush ammonia from an animal's system.

• Proper temperature, lighting and humidity levels, and the absence of stress will go a long way toward preventing illness.

*This arboreal Guatamalan flat-footed salamander, **Dendrotriton rabbi**, relies upon water that collects on the base of the bromeliad upon which it rests.*

• Take care when administering medications, as the mucus-coated skin is the main defense against harmful microorganisms. Damaged skin is often colonized by opportunistic bacteria.

• Handle salamanders infrequently, and always use wet hands or a plastic water-filled bag.

• Nylon nets often damage the skin's mucus covering, opening the way to attack by harmful microorganisms.

• Injection sites (generally a leg) should be noted on a treatment card. The sites should be rotated to avoid overusing a particular one.

Bacteria

Aeromonas hydrophila

This gram negative bacterium is one of the main culprits behind a condition known as *septicemia*. Transmitted by contact with infected water, animals, or substrate, an *Aeromonas* infection typically causes reddish skin hemorrhages that progressively worsen, leading to skin sloughing. Generally, the afflicted animal also decreases its activities, loses weight, and becomes dull in coloration. In its terminal state, the salamander may twitch, convulse, and become comatose.

Although lacerated skin leads one to suspect *Aeromonas,* diagnosis can be made only by blood culture. There is evidence that certain species of frogs may harbor *Aeromonas* bacteria without exhibiting symptoms.

The term *red leg* is often applied to septicemia in amphibians.

In some amphibian species (i.e., Mexican axolotls, *Ambystoma mexicanum,* leopard frogs, *Rana pipiens*), *Aeromonas* infection is often cured by refrigeration at 39 to 41°F (4–5°C) for two weeks.

Salmonella spp.

Salmonella is discussed on page 99 as an "Important Note" in relation to possible hazards to people. An animal afflicted with salmonella

Cautionary Note

Improved sanitation is imperative when dealing with an *Aeromonas* outbreak. Hands must be washed after handling each animal or servicing terrariums.

will generally go off feed, become lethargic and thin, and often develop diarrhea (difficult to observe in salamanders, where waste products are generally in semi-liquid form). A variety of antibiotics has been successfully used against salmonella. Gentamicin, followed by baths in methylene blue and/or *Acriflavine,* is effective.

Mycobacteria spp.

Infection by mycobacteria will manifest as small skin nodules, with the afflicted animal

The unique marked red-legged salamander, **Plethodon shermani,** *is considered a vulnerable species—it is found only on the Unicoi and Nantahala Mountains in North Carolina.*

Adult and juvenile Scott Bar salamanders, **Plethodon asupak.** *The rare species is known only from three creeks in California.*

often developing pneumonia. Afflicted specimens will also usually cease feeding and exhibit abnormal behavior patterns (e.g., lying out in the open). Amikacin and Enrofloxacin are sometimes useful in treatment.

Chlamydia spp.

Chlamydia infection will cause edema, a body-wide swelling unlike the localized abdominal bloat caused by gas. Skin sloughing and hemorrhages, as are often seen in red leg, will appear. Oxytetracycline has proven an effective treatment if administered early.

Gas Bubble Disease

As pertains to amphibians, the term *gas bubble disease* is often used to refer to any one of several related but different maladies. Most commonly, the condition arises when water becomes supersaturated with oxygen, carbon dioxide, or other gases that make up air.

The usual way for a supersaturated condition to occur in captivity is via air introduced through leaks around pumps, tubing, or valves, or via aeration purposely put into the aquarium. In a supersaturated situation, bubbles (emboli) may form in the blood or tissues of the salamander. The bubbles may be seen just below the skin, in the eye, or in the webbing between the toes. They may also congregate in the abdomen, causing it to swell. Death results from the internal accumulation of gas or a secondary bacterial (i.e., *Aeromonas hydrophila*) infection.

Symptoms: Gas bubble disease victims may float and be unable to submerge, and will have trouble feeding and moving about. Eventually, afflicted animals float about on the surface and expire.

The internal bubbles also cause rupturing of capillaries, resulting in sub-skin hemorrhages.

Removing the Gas: Gases may be removed from large systems by allowing water to enter the system via a spray, and then to trickle through 4-foot-high (1.2 m) PVC pipe filled with small stones.

Fungal Infections

Unsanitary environmental conditions and compromised immune systems predispose animals to fungal infections. Diagnosis is accomplished by biopsy, although in some cases symptoms are fairly typical.

Saprolegniasis

Saprolegniasis is one of the more common mycotic infections of aquatic amphibians. The usual culprit is the fungus *Saprolegnia*, although as many as 20 species of aquatic fungi may actually cause the condition.

Saprolegniasis typically manifests as a cottony growth on the animal's skin or gills. The skin below the growth may be inflamed or ulcerated. Victims become weak and thin, seem to have trouble breathing, and may regurgitate.

Cautionary Note

Salamanders are often poisoned after being placed in apparently clean plastic containers that had previously contained soap or other commercial disinfectants.

Saprolegnia is present in most aquatic systems and may begin to cause problems when the mucus on the salamander's skin is removed (e.g., via rough handling) or when the immune system is weakened by stress or disease.

Saprolegnia seems to survive poorly at temperatures over 70°F (21°C). The most effective treatment is benzalkonium chloride.

Parasites

Many parasites are extremely resistant to available medications, with periodic treatments being necessary.

Protozoa exist in a variety of environments and are the causative agents of a tremendous number of diseases in amphibians. Some, such as *Trypanosoma diemictyli*, are always fatal and not treatable at the present time. *Charchesium* and *Vorticella* cause a fuzzy covering on the gills and will kill the animal by preventing proper respiration. A bath in distilled water for two to three hours and in a 0.6 percent sodium chloride solution for three to five days has proven effective, as have copper sulfate treatments.

Velvet Disease

Velvet disease is caused by a flagellated protozoan known as *Oodinium pillularis*. Generally, the disease begins as a small fuzzy gray area on

The attractive red-cheeked salamander, **Plethodon jordani,** *lives at fairly high elevations in the American Southeast.*

the skin or gills. If the disease concentrates on the gills, the animal will be seen gulping for air. A distilled water bath for two to three hours followed by a sodium chloride bath for three to five days (0.6 percent solution) or treatment with copper sulfate is recommended.

Calcium:Phosphorus Ratio

A calcium:phosphorus ratio of less than 1.2:1 may lead to deformed or soft bones. The animal will also be subject to fractures and, in advanced stages, will exhibit tetany (inability to right, twitching toes and limbs). At this stage calcium gluconate injections are the only means of effecting a cure. In the early stages, supplementation with calcium carbonate will help to prevent or reverse the process.

Vitamin D Imbalance

In contrast to many reptiles, salamanders do not bask in order to synthesize vitamin D in the skin. In fact, chemicals providing protection against ultraviolet light have been found in the eggs and skins of certain species, indicating that at least certain wavelengths of UV radiation may be harmful to them. A varied diet and vitamin supplements will help meet their vitamin D requirements.

Chemicals and Other Substances

Chlorine, ammonia, pesticides, disinfectants, and many other compounds can injure or kill salamanders. If the local water supply system has copper, zinc, or lead pipes, water should be allowed to run for up to half an hour before being used. Spring water baths can be used to help detoxify animals that have been exposed to chemical poisoning.

Rock, wood, and cork bark may also absorb and retain harmful chemicals. Cleaning and disinfecting is best done by using very hot water and salt or bleach. Bleach rinses readily and more completely than other cleaners. A few drops of commercial instant water dechlorinator (available at pet stores) should be used to assure that all has dissipated.

OBTAINING SALAMANDERS

Although in general people should refrain from collecting salamanders, there are instances when populations in areas slated for development escape the notice of state and other regulatory agencies. Red tape, inappropriate surveys, and lack of funding can all combine to leave such populations doomed to extinction.

Concerned naturalists who collect such animals are performing an invaluable service. Where possible, their activities should be carried out in cooperation with a nature center, zoo, museum, or government body.

Zoos, Museums, Pet Stores, and Other Institutions

Zoos lack the space to adequately address amphibian conservation, and therefore sometimes form cooperative breeding agreements with serious nonprofessionals. Government confiscations of animals illegally put into

Salamanders should not be kept in crowded conditions. These are marbled newts, Triturus marmoratus.

the food or pet trade currently account for a significant portion of the unexpected animals with which zoos must deal each year. In limited circumstances, these animals may be sent to private individuals while trials are pending or for permanent placement. Incorporation into this process is most easily attained by involvement with serious herpetological organizations, zoos, and museums.

It is important to establish a good working relationship with the pet store or private breeder with whom you deal. This will enable you to ascertain necessary background information about specimens in which you are interested. Reputable stores and dealers know the importance of such information and should be happy to provide it.

Unlike other tiger salamanders, with which it was formerly classified, **Ambystoma mavortium nebulosum** *is not boldly marked in yellow and black.*

Choosing an Individual

The sex of the individual is important, but is not always determinable outside of the breeding season. (Please see species descriptions for specifics.)

Animals should be well fed but not obese. Check above the hips to determine whether an animal is too thin; noticeable bones there usually indicate that an animal is underfed. This is especially useful for species that are very thinly built.

Bloat: One also needs to distinguish between an animal with a full stomach and one that is bloated. Bloating commonly appears as a swelling along the sides and in the stomach area. Edema is indicated by generalized swelling and, for aquatic species, difficulty in swimming.

Background Information: Background information should be obtained on the individual that you wish to purchase. This is vital for breeding purposes, and it is especially important in terms of the animal's range. Many salamander species are broken into widely distributed populations, the unique characteristics of which may be preserved by breeding only with animals from the same population.

Salamanders kept in an overcrowded situation should be avoided, as the problems they likely have are undetectable through casual observation. For example, removal of the slime coating caused by rubbing against walls and other animals in crowded conditions usually results in bacterial infections.

Laws and Regulations

An offer for sale does not guarantee legality, nor does the fact that the individual was captive bred. If you are unsure, call your state Department of Environmental Conservation or equivalent agency.

The Ideal Situation— Studying Wild Populations

Natural populations of salamanders tend to be very stable in terms of their location, and studying them in many ways resembles the captive situation. However, nothing compares to actually going out and learning about these creatures in the wild. Little is known about the life histories of even the most widespread species—particularly lacking are studies that span the entire year.

Herpetologists are usually underfunded and may welcome competent assistance in the field. Speak to local nature centers, zoos, and universities to determine who is working in your area, and make yourself available. Many of the details of fieldwork can be accomplished by nonprofessionals and will add greatly to the store of information being collected on free-living individuals.

One of several subspecies of the painted ensatina salamander, Ensatina eschscholtzii platensis.

Preliminary Considerations

Transportation and shipping are extremely stressful situations for newts and salamanders. Relocation weakens the immune system and microorganisms that are relatively harmless to animals living in stress-free situations, suddenly become capable of causing life-threatening infections .

Bear in mind also that most salamanders naturally occupy discrete territories in the wild—a change in habitat leaves them without any sense of security. As such usually happens several times in quick succession when a salamander enters the pet trade (collection or removal from breeding enclosure, transfer to dealer or importer, shipment to store, transfer to new owner, etc.), it pays to take extra care when moving and establishing new animals.

Transportation Containers

Plastic bags make ideal transportation containers for aquatic salamanders, and pillowcases function well for terrestrial species. Be sure to turn pillowcases inside out, as threads within the cases may entangle the occupants' legs. Newspaper should be packed tightly around all shipping containers, even if a short trip is involved—an enclosure that moves about is the equivalent of an earthquake to a salamander or newt!

Avoid using glass, plastic, or screen containers, as animals in transit often attempt to escape, and will injure their delicate skins.

Shelters

Newts and salamanders should be able to hide within transport containers.

Plastic shelters should not be used in transportation containers because they can move about and cause injuries. Sphagnum moss is ideal for terrestrial salamanders, as they can burrow into the moss and it is nonabrasive and retains moisture well.

Newts and aquatic salamanders will fare well in shallow water provisioned with live or plastic plants. Be sure that floating plants are available so that newts in transit are able to rest.

Controlling Temperature

The transportation container should be packed inside a food cooler so that temperature can be controlled. In the rare event that additional warmth is necessary, a hot water bottle or hand-warming packet can be used. Freezer packs wrapped in newspaper serve well to lower temperatures.

A pillowcase partially filled with sphagnum moss makes an effective carrier for terrestrial species. Use a sturdy plastic bag partially filled with water for aquatic species.

Prior to transporting salamanders, be sure to experiment with temperature-controlling methods in the cooler that you will be using. This will enable you to determine how much heating or cooling element to use and how long its effectiveness is retained.

Quarantine and Fecal Exams

Animals new to your collection should be quarantined before being placed with others. This will allow you to observe peculiarities of their feeding and behavior, and to monitor their health.

The standard procedure in zoological parks is to keep new animals separated from the main collection until three fecal samples have been shown negative for parasites. If you have access to a veterinarian experienced in amphibian care, this procedure, or even a single fecal test, is very worthwhile.

If fecal exams are not performed, a quarantine of at least one month should be instituted.

Feeding

If the new salamander does not actively feed while you are watching, use a food source that is easy to count and simple for the animal to find. In this regard, crickets, which remain on the surface, or waxworms, which can be confined to a bowl, are preferable to burrowing invertebrates. Simply designed quarantine terrariums will ease fecal collection and observation, but these considerations must be weighed against the animal's need for a secure, naturalistic environment.

When considering the diet of newly acquired animals, be aware that salamanders, especially wild-caught individuals, can become fixated on specific prey items. Also, they may enter cycles or phases when they will prefer one type of food

A Styrofoam cooler and freezer packs or a hot water bottle will enable you to maintain proper temperatures during transportation.

to another. This might be linked to availability in the wild, or perhaps it is a method of assuring proper nutrition.

Observations

Disturb your new acquisition as little as possible, and experiment with a variety of foods. This is especially important early on, as observations are more easily conducted when animals are housed singly. In a community situation, detailed observations will be more difficult. Commercially available night-viewing bulbs will help you to watch shy, nocturnal salamanders.

Earthworms will live well in cool sphagnum moss or soil. Secretive salamanders will capture them during the evening, assuming that the worms cannot burrow completely out of reach. Earthworms will also survive for 24 to 48 hours in well-aerated water, allowing aquatic species that will not feed while you are present the chance to eat.

NATURAL HISTORY AND CARE OF VARIOUS SPECIES

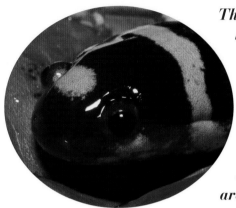

The incredible variety of salamander lifestyles—aquatic to terrestrial, fossorial to arboreal—largely precludes the establishment of general rules pertaining to captive husbandry. It is, therefore, vital that you carefully research the natural history and captive care of those species in which you are interested.

Ambystomatidae

Mexican Axolotl
(*Ambystoma mexicanum*)

Range and Habitat: This aquatic relative of the familiar tiger and spotted salamanders is nearly extinct in the wild. Originally, its entire natural habitat consisted of Lake Xochimilco and Lake Chalco, both along the southern edge of Mexico City. Collection for food, habitat loss, and pollution have now limited the axolotl to the southern remnants of Lake Xochimilco and several associated canals and private ponds, an area that covers a mere 6.2 square miles.

Although the wild axolotl has long been an important research animal, the first study of it

A blackchin red salamander, **Pseudotriton ruber schenchi,** *in the author's collection is approaching 30 years of age.*

appears to have commenced in the mid-1980s. There is a good deal of confusion about species integrity because Mexican axolotls interbreed with the neotenic stages of tiger salamanders. In fact, this appears to have happened among the original specimens that were sent to Europe for study.

The importance of axolotls in developmental biology and embryology research has resulted in the establishment of huge captive populations, but the genetic makeup of these individuals is uncertain. Animals offered for sale in the pet trade are almost certainly captive bred.

Description: Wild axolotls are olive brown with branching reddish gills, but leucistic, albino, black, yellow, piebald, and even fluorescent strains have been developed in captivity.

Lifestyle: The completely aquatic axolotl is termed an *inducible obligate neotene*. This means that the natural situation is for it to be

A normally-colored Mexican axolotl, **Ambystoma mexicanum.** *A variety of color strains have been produced in captivity.*

neotenic, that is, to retain larval characteristics such as external gills. However, metamorphosis can be induced by manipulating the function of the thyroid gland. This is in contrast to relatives such as tiger salamanders, *Ambystoma tigrinum,* which are termed *facultative neotenes.* In these species, transformation to the adult form usually occurs, but in some circumstances, the animals will reproduce in the larval form.

Care: The axolotl makes a fairly hardy aquarium animal and is a good species upon which to sharpen one's breeding skills. Its natural habitat is at a high elevation where the water is always cool. Mexican axolotls fare best at temperatures below 70°F (19°C), with a drop to 52°F (10°C) during the winter.

Although they can be slowly acclimated to a variety of water types, axolotls do best in soft water with a pH of 6.9 to 7.6.

In contrast to most salamanders, axolotls do fine without any shelter. They will respond to people by swimming to the surface if they are accustomed to eating floating food. In crowded tanks, the presence of shelters will help to alleviate aggression between the animals.

Breeding: Adults are sexually dimorphic. Females are of a heavier build than males, have short, broad heads, and become noticeably swollen with eggs during the breeding season. The cloaca of the male swells during the breeding season and protrudes to a greater extent than does that of the female throughout the rest of the year.

A drop in temperature will stimulate reproduction. A cool basement is ideal for keeping axolotls year-round, as the natural fluctuations in temperature (and possibly of light entering windows, if any) will be enough to stimulate normal reproduction. Axolotls remain fairly seasonal in their breeding, laying eggs from January through March or April. A sudden increase of water volume, however, may stimulate reproduction outside of the normal breeding season.

Breeding males secrete pheromones to attract females, who butt the males with their snouts about the cloacal region. The male releases a pyramidal spermatophore and then leads the female, who continues to maintain snout contact with his cloaca, over the spermatophore. Females have been observed to pick up several spermatophores nightly.

Eggs: Axolotl eggs are attached to water plants or any other substrate within the tank. Adults are ravenous consumers of their own eggs, and should therefore be removed after spawning.

At temperatures of 55 to 60°F (11.5–14°C), axolotl eggs will hatch within two to three weeks. The eggs should be incubated with mild aeration, just enough to keep them slightly moving. Eggs attached to plants and floating objects seem to have a higher hatch rate than do those deposited along the bottom of the aquarium.

Larvae: Larvae begin feeding about one day after hatching, the first day being spent motionless on the bottom of the tank. Newly hatched brine shrimp and very finely chopped blackworms are accepted.

Axolotl larvae will also feed upon each other if not given plenty of room and lots of cover. Bare-bottom tanks are best for raising the larvae. At a size of approximately 2 inches (5 cm) in length (and sometimes earlier), they will begin to take trout chow, Reptomin, and other prepared foods. Reptomin and other prepared foods, along with occasional earthworms, blackworms, and small fishes, provide an excellent diet for these animals.

When feeding blackworms be aware that axolotl larvae will attempt to engulf large balls of worms, and may choke (both chopped and whole blackworms congregate into small balls).

Live foods stimulate feeding frenzies among axolotls, and many individuals will routinely grab the gills and toes of their tank-mates. Generally these grow back without problems, but a treatment with Stress Coat or Novaqua is recommended to prevent infection.

*White axolotls, **Ambystoma mexicanum**, are common in the pet trade.*

Marbled Salamander
(*Ambystoma opacum*)

Range and Habitat: The marbled salamander ranges from southern New England to northern Florida, and west to southern Illinois, eastern Oklahoma, and eastern Texas.

The marbled salamander is a terrestrial creature as an adult and inhabits woodlands and, to a lesser extent, fields and moist, sandy areas.

Description: The marbled salamander is a member of the family Ambystomatidae, the mole salamanders. True to the family name, this attractively patterned creature spends most of its life underground, either in burrows of its own making or sheltering within those made by rodents or invertebrates.

It is a small but strikingly marked creature. The adult size is 3½ to 4½ inches (9–11 cm). The background of the animal is black, and it is marked with cross-bands, often in an hourglass shape, along the entire body. These are white or grayish—generally whiter on the male and grayer on the female—and they contrast sharply with the animal's jet black background. Like the others in its family, it is sturdily built, and gives the appearance of being larger.

Care: Marbled salamanders make fairly hardy captives. In the terrarium it will use the same burrow for years, emerging only at night and often staying near the entrance. However, well-habituated individuals can be induced to feed during the day and may relinquish their burrowing ways and take up residence in artificial caves and the like.

Small earthworms, blackworms, ¼-to-½-inch (6–13 mm) crickets, sow bugs, and other small invertebrates are readily accepted. In the wild, marbled salamanders do not require standing

The light bands of the male marbled salamander are of a brighter hue than those of the female.

A female marbled salamander guarding her eggs.

water outside of the breeding season, but a shallow water bowl should be provided in captivity.

Substrate can be fashioned from soil, dead leaves, peat moss, and sphagnum. If allowed to form deep, permanent burrow systems, a variety of interesting behaviors might be observed. Blocking the back of the terrarium, so that all burrowing is confined along the front glass, or covering the glass with easily removable black paper will facilitate observations.

Breeding: In contrast to all other family members, marbled salamanders lay their eggs in the fall, on land. The female remains with the eggs in a small depression that has been hollowed out under dead leaves or a fallen log. The nest is situated along the sides of an ephemeral (temporary) pool. Although dry at the time of egg laying, these pools fill with water during winter thaws or spring rains.

The eggs hatch at that time, and the larvae begin feeding on fairy shrimp or other small invertebrates that are active even during the colder months.

Larger, related species such as tiger and spotted salamanders often use the same breeding pools as marbled salamanders. By the time their eggs hatch later in the spring, the marbled salamander larvae have already grown significantly, and are able to include their newly hatched relatives in their diet.

Captive breeding requires a winter cooling period and a simulation of the very specific breeding habitat. If one is fortunate enough to obtain fertile eggs, they should be left with the female for approximately six weeks to two months, at which time water should be added

until it reaches the level of the eggs. Hatching should occur quickly at that time.

Larvae: The larvae are predisposed to fast growth and require a good deal of food. Upon hatching, they are only about 1/2 inch (13 mm) long and will take newly hatched brine shrimp, *Infusoria*, and finely chopped blackworms. Eventually, blackworms can form the basis of the diet, supplemented occasionally with tiny earthworms.

The larvae will prey upon each other unless given plenty of room and cover. They average 2.4 to 3.2 inches (6–8 cm) long upon transformation to the terrestrial form, and become sexually mature when just over one year old.

Tiger Salamander (*Ambystoma tigrinum*)

Range and Habitat: This member of the family Ambystomatidae (the mole salamanders), is the world's largest land-dwelling salamander. The record length for the eastern race, *A. t. tigrinum*, is 13 inches (33 cm).

It also has the greatest range of any North American salamander, occurring from extreme

The Eastern tiger salamander, **Ambystoma tigrinum tigrinum,** *may exceed 12 inches in length.*

southeastern Alaska east to the southern part of Labrador and south throughout the entire United States to the southern edge of the Mexican Plateau.

Some of the discussion concerning other members of the family Ambystomatidae can be applied to the tiger salamander, but this animal is unique and makes a long-lived and interesting captive.

Adults lead a terrestrial existence and may inhabit forests, grasslands, or marshy areas. One general requirement seems to be soil in which they are able to burrow or in which the burrows of other species of animals might be used.

Kin Recognition

Studies have indicated that tiger salamander larvae prefer to prey upon nonrelated animals, exhibiting a type of kin recognition.

Although well suited for terrestrial existence, tiger salamanders do need to be able to go underground to seek the proper humidity levels. During dry periods, large numbers of tiger salamanders have been found lying in piles in burrows and beneath suitable cover.

Description: Adult tiger salamanders are thick-bodied creatures. Their coloration, generally yellow blotches, spots, or bars against a jet black background, is quite stunning. Occasionally, the blotches and spots are gold to olive green in color. The size, shape, quantity, and position of the blotches varies among individuals within a population and among populations.

The tiger salamander's broad head houses a mouth capable of taking prey to the size of a small mouse. There are tubercles at the bottom of the feet and hands that seem to assist in digging.

Care: As both larvae and adults, tiger salamanders are voracious feeders, with adults tending to become obese in captivity. Captive tiger salamanders exhibit an unusual degree of alertness and boldness. They will completely abandon their secretive ways, prowling about in the daytime when hungry. Most feed readily from the hand, and they can often be brought out of hiding by a slight tapping on the glass. If fed after this, they will soon make the association and respond each time.

Because of their large size, it is easy to provide a well-balanced diet. Earthworms, crickets, and waxworms can make up the bulk of the diet, but sow bugs, beetles, and other wild-caught invertebrates should be added on occasion.

Tiger salamanders will readily consume pink mice, and in the wild they may occasionally stumble upon a field-mouse nest and consume the young. However, a steady diet of such in captivity soon leads to health problems.

Adults can be housed in a woodland terrarium, and semi-permanent burrows will be dug and used. They also thrive in simple, easily cleaned enclosures with a sphagnum or paper towel substrate, artificial cave, and water bowl.

Breeding: Tiger salamanders breed quite early in the year and during very cold weather. On Long Island, New York, they often move to breeding ponds during warm spells in January, and eggs have been found in February.

Breeding takes place in the water. Generally, many males surround one or two females. A receptive female will allow the male to push her away from the group, often seemingly balanced upon his snout. Once she has been separated from the other males, the successful male will head-butt the female's cloaca region and then walk before her while brushing her snout with his tail.

If all goes well, the female will follow the male, pushing against his cloaca with her snout, at which point he will release the sperm package, or spermatophore. The spermatophore is taken into the female's cloaca by the cloacal lips, thereby allowing for internal fertilization. Egg-laying generally begins within a few hours.

The globular egg mass is attached to submerged branches or aquatic vegetation. Many clusters containing 20–100 eggs are laid over the course of several days, with especially large females laying up to 5,000 eggs.

During the remainder of the year tiger salamanders shelter deep within self-dug burrows or those made by moles and other small mammals.

Larvae: The cannibalistic larvae are an important source of food for other creatures in the pond.

Tiger salamander larvae may recognize their siblings, and usually choose unrelated individuals as prey.

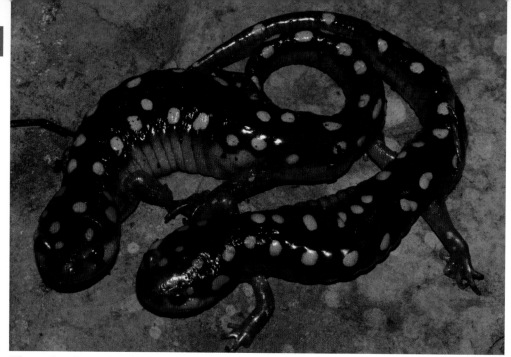

The strikingly-patterned spotted salamander, **Ambystoma maculatum,** *makes a fine terrarium subject.*

As water levels drop in ephemeral (temporary) breeding ponds, certain larvae develop broader heads and larger teeth than other larvae. These animals then begin feeding ravenously upon less well-armed larvae, and consequently grow more quickly than they would on the more typical diet of small invertebrates.

Because their rapid growth allows for early transformation, these more aggressive larvae are able to enter the land phase before the pond dries up. In captivity, removing one-eighth to one-quarter of the water each day often causes an almost immediate onset of gill loss and transformation to adult form.

Certain larvae can grow to quite large sizes, 8 to 10 inches (20.3–25.4 cm), and not exhibit signs of transformation for several years. Tiger salamander populations in parts of the Pacific Northwest and Mexico exhibit neoteny, and

breed in the larval form. The adult terrestrial stage is completely lacking. Such larvae may reach 11 inches (30 cm) in length.

Spotted Salamander (*Ambystoma maculatum*)

Range and Habitat: This brightly marked salamander is related to the tiger salamander and follows a similar life cycle. It ranges from southern Ontario to Georgia, and west to eastern Texas, but is absent from much of southern New Jersey and the Delmarva Peninsula.

Adults generally frequent forested areas, where they may be found within rotting logs or, more commonly, underground in self-dug burrows or those abandoned by small mammals.

Description: The spotted salamander is a stoutly built creature and reaches 5 to 7 inches (12.7–17.7 cm) in length (record 9¼ inches

[24.8 cm]). Adults are jet or bluish black with rows of irregular yellow or occasionally orange spots. Rare individuals lack spots altogether.

Care: The spotted salamander will feed upon blackworms, earthworms, waxworms, small crickets, sow bugs, millipedes, and other invertebrates. Habituated animals may leave their shelters and actively seek food during the day. In general, however, they are secretive creatures and are best observed with as little disturbance as possible. Wild adults do not use standing water except for breeding, but captives should be provided a shallow water dish.

As with the tiger salamander, captive breeding requires a winter cooling period.

Breeding: In southern New York, spotted salamanders generally breed around the third week of March. At this time the water is quite cold, with adults sometimes crossing snow to reach their breeding ponds.

The sexes arrive at the ponds separately, the males first and the females with the next warming rain. Many are killed by cars at this time, and others fall into drainage sumps and perish.

In some locales, volunteer patrols and road closings during the breeding season, and specially designed tunnels, have resulted in substantial reductions in the number of road-killed spotted salamanders.

Larvae: The reproductive process is similar to that described for the tiger salamander. The larvae are approximately 1/2 inch (13 mm) long upon hatching, and leave the breeding ponds within their first summer at 2.4 inches (6 cm) in length.

The globular egg mass of the spotted salamander is attached to submerged sticks and plants.

Plethodontidae

Northern Dusky Salamander (*Desmognathus fuscus*)

Range and Habitat: The northern dusky salamander ranges from southern New Brunswick and Quebec to Louisiana. It and related subspecies are usually confined to wet areas along clear, flowing creeks and streams.

Description: Lacking gills or lungs, dusky salamanders rely upon cutaneous respiration and are therefore restricted to moist environments. They are quite agile, and can move over land and swim with great speed and agility.

The northern dusky salamander, one of the largest species in the genus, may reach 7.2 inches (18 cm) in length. *Desmognathus aeneus*, the smallest, matures when a mere 1.6 inches (4 cm) long.

Most individuals are some shade of brown with a light stripe down the center and a light

band from the eye to the corner of the mouth, but there is much variation in this regard.

Care: The northern dusky salamander should be kept in a moist terrarium with a water section and a substrate of peat, sphagnum, and/or carpet moss. Hiding spots are essential, and temperatures should be maintained at or below 65°F (18°C).

Breeding: Individuals to be bred must be subjected to a hibernation period. The last meal should be about ten days before hibernation, at which time the temperature may slowly be lowered to about 43°F (6°C). Dusky salamanders can be overwintered in wet sphagnum moss.

As with many lungless salamanders, courting males rub the submandibular gland (in the lower jaw) over the female's head and dorsal surface. Females have been observed rubbing the males' tails with their front legs in response. Eventually, the male dusky salamander releases a spermatophore, which the female takes into her cloaca.

Six to eight weeks later the female deposits 10 to 40 eggs in a moist, secluded shelter below a log. She stays wrapped about the eggs for the four-to-six-week incubation period, possibly to prevent desiccation and protect them from invertebrate predators.

Larvae: In an unusual twist to typical salamander larval development, the ½ inch (13 mm) long larvae remain in the nest cavity for approximately two weeks, and then move to the water where external gills develop. They transform into the terrestrial adult form in seven to ten months, depending on range and temperature. Sexual maturity is believed to be reached in three years.

Dusky salamanders feed upon earthworms, slugs, and leaf litter invertebrates. Pinhead crickets, aphids, fruit flies, and chopped blackworms are suitable for newly transformed captives.

Green Salamander (*Aneides aeneus*)

Range: The green salamander is restricted to the Appalachian Mountains in southwestern Pennsylvania, western Maryland, northeastern Mississippi, and the region spanning southern Ohio to central Alabama, with a disjunct population in southwestern North Carolina.

Description: This is the only green-colored North American salamander. The background color is mottled with darker blotches that resemble patches of lichen. The green salamander is typically found among rock piles, and has squared-off toe tips, which may assist in climbing.

Care: Flat shale over a damp substrate of sphagnum moss makes an ideal captive habitat for this salamander. It is a particularly adept climber, so the terrarium's lid must be well secured.

Because the green salamander reaches only 3 to 5 inches (7.2–12 cm) in length, its food should consist of ¼-inch (6 mm) crickets, small earthworms, blackworms, and tiny waxworms, as well as wild-caught sow bugs, millipedes, and other leaf litter invertebrates.

Maintaining Moisture

Green salamanders most often choose to shelter within rock crevices. Those in the terrarium should be misted daily so that moisture accumulates therein. Moss wedged between the rock slabs helps maintain adequate moisture.

The green salamander, **Aneides aeneus.** *Note its lichen-like camouflage and square toes, which assist in climbing.*

Breeding: In the spring, the green salamander lays 10–20 stalked eggs on land. They are guarded by the female until autumn, at which time small, fully developed salamanders emerge.

Red-Backed Salamander (*Plethodon cinereus*)

This tiny creature (Family Plethodontidae) relies entirely on oxygen transfer through its skin for respiration, and is considered among the most terrestrial of all salamanders.

Range and Habitat: The red-backed salamander occurs from southern Quebec to Minnesota, and south to North Carolina and Missouri, and can reach high densities in favorable habitats. In northeastern forests, its biomass typically exceeds that of all other vertebrates combined, despite an adult size of merely 2 to 4 inches (5–10 cm) in length.

Their importance to the overall functioning of the ecosystem can thus not be overstressed.

It is, therefore, quite alarming that they are becoming harder to find in many areas, with rain-acidified soil being considered a major culprit.

Description: The red-backed salamander is extremely variable in coloration, both throughout its range and among individuals within the same habitat. Usually, a red or reddish dorsal stripe down the center of the back is exhibited, but some have light gray stripes or dark gray or black backs (these are generally referred to as lead-backed salamanders).

Red-backed salamanders seem to possess strong skin toxins that discourage many predators. In the presence of a potential predator, the animal elevates and lashes its tail back and forth. Stressed red-backed salamanders will also

The red-backed salamander, **Plethodon cinereus,** *has neither gills nor lungs, and breathes through its skin.*

drop the tail, which remains wiggling for some time, and may bite at small snakes and other predators seeking to consume them.

Care: Even fully grown adults are incapable of taking anything but quite small prey. One-quarter-inch (6 mm) crickets, blackworms, and tiny earthworms can form the basis of the diet. Complex, well-planted terrariums can be created so that natural patterns of territoriality might be observed.

Red-backed salamanders pile feces at the edges of their territory. Cleaning should be regulated so as to leave a bit of this to help preserve natural behaviors among mating animals. A very large, well-planted terrarium with a few animals, that need not be broken down and completely cleaned, is ideal.

Breeding: Red-backed salamanders are extremely territorial. Males apparently mark their territory with small piles of fecal material; females investigate these, apparently using olfaction to determine the diet and fitness of the male.

Upon choosing a mate, the female will enter his territory, whereupon he will push her with his snout and nip at her. He then sequentially raises and lowers each leg in front of her while pushing his snout against her throat region and moving below her. The animals then walk together with body and tail in contact, the male on the bottom, the female above. At some point he deposits a spermatophore, which is taken up by the female.

Eggs: Only 3 to 11 individual eggs are laid—far fewer than most species. Constant parental care ensures a fairly high hatch rate. The eggs are generally attached to the ceiling of a small depression below a log or rock. The female remains with the eggs, curled about them to prevent desiccation and driving off small predators. There is some evidence that the female will remove eggs that have developed fungus.

This red-backed salamander is unusually bright in coloration.

Larvae: In contrast to many salamanders, the young hatch out as perfectly formed miniatures of the adult. They do have tiny external gills that are absorbed within a few days, but in all other respects the larval stage is skipped. Sexual maturity is reached in about 18 months.

Northern Red Salamander (*Pseudotriton ruber ruber*)

Range and Habitat: The northern red salamander ranges from southern New York west to Ohio and south to northern Alabama. Its activities are restricted almost entirely to the very wet areas along the banks of running streams. Red salamanders are never found near stagnant water, and seem even more sensitive to water quality and temperature than other salamanders.

Description: Most red salamanders are about 5 inches (12.7 cm) long, although some individuals exceed 7 inches (17.8 cm) in length. The brilliant red background is highlighted by jet black

Northern red salamanders (Pseudotriton ruber ruber) *in their natural habitat.*

flecks along the back and the legs. As the animals mature, the red tends to fade, with older animals being a dark purple or reddish brown in color.

Care: Captive longevity approaches 30 years, but red salamanders fail to thrive unless all details of proper care are adhered to. Although not aquatic, they do tend to spend more time

The rarely seen black-chinned red salamander, Pseudotriton ruber schrencki, is closely related to the Northern red salamander.

should be maintained at or below 65°F (18°C). The people most successful with this species often maintain them in terrariums stored within large coolers provisioned with ice packs.

Red salamanders have fairly small mouths, so food items must be sized accordingly. They relish blackworms, small earthworms, 1/4-to-1/2-inch (6–13 mm) crickets, tiny waxworms, termites, sow bugs, and leaf litter invertebrates.

Breeding: A winter cooling period at 40°F (4°C) seems necessary to stimulate reproduction and would most likely assist the animals' overall health. The eggs, which are guarded by the female, are laid on land under flat rocks or within damp, rotting logs along streams. There is often a long larval period, sometimes in excess of two and a half years.

in the water than do the more terrestrial members of their family. An ideal setup would be a large terrarium planted with moss over gravel and equipped with a shallow water section filtered by a submersible filter. Temperatures

The brilliantly-colored Northern red salamander, Pseudotriton ruber ruber, may live for over 30 years in captivity.

Four spring salamander subspecies inhabit eastern North America. This is the brightly colored **Gyrinophilus porphyritcus danielsi.**

Related Species: The eastern mud salamander, *Pseudotriton montanus montanus*, is closely related to the red salamander and similar in appearance. The two may be distinguished by eye color, the mud salamander's being brown and the red salamander's yellow.

Their habitats are also different. Mud salamanders dwell along the muddy sections of slow-moving creeks, where they appear to make use of crayfish burrows. They can be kept in a manner similar to the red salamander, and are equally as shy and as sensitive to high temperatures.

Spring Salamander (*Gyrinophilus porphyriticus*)

Range and Habitat: There are two very different species within the genus *Gyrinophilus*.

The spring salamander (*Gyrinophilus porphyriticus*) ranges from Quebec and southern Maine to Georgia, Alabama, and Mississippi, and exists as a complex of four subspecies. It is semi-aquatic, and apparently restricted to cool, wet areas along shallow mountain streams.

The aquatic Tennessee cave salamander, *Gyrinophilus palleucus*, is neotenic, and known only from caves within central and southeastern Tennessee, northern Alabama, and northwestern Georgia.

Description: The spring salamander is quite variable but always startling in coloration. The background can be salmon, pink, reddish, or orange-yellow, and there are usually black flecks on the dorsal surface. It grows to a length of 7½ inches (19 cm), and is an extremely delicate captive.

This spring salamander, Gyrinophilus palleucus necturoides, *is limited in distribution to Kentucky's Big Mouth Cave.*

Breeding: Mating occurs in the fall, and the eggs are laid the following spring and sometimes into summer, depending upon the elevation in which the animal is living.

Subspecies: Several subspecies each generally limited to one cave or cave system, have been identified, including the Sinking Cave salamander, *G.p. pallecus*, and the Big Mouth Cave salamander, *G.p. necturoides*. Because much of their range and habitat is underground, none have been thoroughly studied.

One former subspecies, the Berry Cave salamander, has recently been reclassified as a distinct species, *G. gulolineatus*.

Salamandridae

Spanish Ribbed Newt
(*Pleurodeles waltl*)

Range: The Spanish ribbed newt is native to the southwestern portion of the Iberian Peninsula and northwestern Morocco.

Description: This largest of Europe's newts (to 12 inches, 30 cm) is dark olive with blackish spots. When threatened, the ribbed newt will push its rib tips against the skin, thus elevating the poison glands there. The tips of the ribs are sharp and may pierce the skin without harming the newt. The head of the Spanish ribbed newt is more flattened than that of other newts, and

The stout Spanish ribbed newt, Pleurodeles waltl, *thrusts poison tipped ribs through its skin when threatened.*

Ribbed newts utilize a unique mode of amplexus, with the male grasping the female from below.

the tail is laterally compressed to assist in swimming. The species is largely aquatic, leaving the water for short periods to rest.

Care: In the terrarium, Spanish ribbed newts should be provided with a land area and shallow water with floating plants. They're not particularly strong swimmers despite their size, so filtration outflow should be mild. In the wild state, they remain active throughout the year, but may pass dry periods buried in mud.

Like many aquatic newts, the Spanish ribbed newt will take pelleted food as well as crickets, earthworms, blackworms, shrimp, and minnows.

Breeding: In both the wild and captivity, the Spanish ribbed newt may breed throughout the year, whenever conditions are favorable. Reproductively active males develop swollen, roughened areas of skin, known as nuptial pads, along the inner sides of the two front legs. Courtship occurs in water, with the male moving below the female and rubbing his head against her throat. In a somewhat unusual courtship position, he then grips her forearms from below with his forearms.

At some point the male will deposit a small spermatophore near the female's head, and he will then turn and position her so that she can pick up the spermatophore with her cloaca. The eggs are deposited in clumps on submerged branches and plants approximately one month after mating.

Larvae: Larvae hatch within one to two weeks, depending on temperature, and can be raised on chopped blackworms and brine shrimp.

Marbled Newt
(*Triturus marmoratus*)

Range: The two subspecies of marbled newt are found in southwestern France and the Iberian Peninsula.

Description: Marbled newts can reach a length of 6.4 inches (16 cm), although most are somewhat smaller than that. They differ in color from most of the other members of the genus in that their backs are mottled in an attractive green-and-black pattern. However, other color combinations, including yellow and brown, have been observed.

In common with the other nine species within the genus *Triturus,* the marbled newt enters the water after its winter hibernation period. Tails of both subspecies flatten out a bit to allow for swimming, and those of the male develop to a greater extent as a secondary sex characteristic.

The marbled newt, **Triturus marmoratus,** *is one of the most attractively colored of all European amphibians.*

Care: Marbled newts can be kept in a terrestrial setup during most of the year, and after hibernation moved into an aquatic habitat. The change in terrarium environment seems to stimulate breeding.

Warm temperatures are to be strictly avoided; 72°F (22°C) is about the highest that these animals can tolerate. During the winter, temperatures should be allowed to drop to between 36 and 46°F (2–8°C). The daylight period should be shortened at this time so that a pattern similar to that of the temperate latitudes in which they live is followed. Overwintering should occur in damp moss.

Blackworms, small earthworms, crickets, waxworms, and small insects make up the adult diet. Larvae can be raised on brine shrimp and finely chopped blackworms.

Marbled newts, and the larvae in particular, are very sensitive to water quality, so strict attention should be paid to cleanliness in their aquarium.

Breeding: Males in breeding condition follow females, apparently analyzing any pheromones released to determine receptivity. Courting males position themselves in front of the female and release pheromones designed to stimulate the female to pick up the spermatophore. The tip of the male's tail is waved while the spermatophores are being released, possibly to create a current that carries the scent toward the female. The spermatophore is generally deposited after the female makes contact with the male's tail or body with her snout. Courting males manipulate the female so that she comes into contact with the spermatophore.

Fertilized females lay eggs at various times throughout the next two to three months, with a total of up to 200 eventually being deposited. Each is laid singly on a water plant, and the female bends the tip of the plant's leaf over the egg to form a covering. The eggs should be removed to a separate aquarium as they are laid, lest they be consumed by the adult newts.

Hatching occurs within two to three weeks, and the young newts transform by the end of the first summer.

Larvae: The larvae follow the typical newt pattern of development, moving onto moist land as they lose their gills. They can be raised in a damp terrarium with a small water section until they are two to three years old, at which time sexual maturity occurs.

Although faster growth may occur if the animals are kept active all year, these and most other salamanders should ideally be subjected to a winter period even during their growth years. Keeping them on a natural temperature and light cycle may help to encourage normal breeding upon maturity.

Eastern Newt (*Notophthalmus viridescens*)

Range: The Eastern newts consist of a complex of several subspecies within the family Salamandridae. The widest-ranging subspecies, the red-spotted newt (*N. v. viridescens*), occurs from Canada's Maritime Provinces west to the Great Lakes and south to central Georgia.

Description: This newt, which grows to a size of 4 inches (10 cm) and occasionally longer, is generally found in and around quiet waters supporting a good deal of plant growth. Depending upon the range and subspecies, they are dark brown to tan in color with red dots

that may be encircled by black. Some subspecies exhibit broken or continuous red stripes along the dorsal surface. The abdomen is yellow to orange.

Adult males develop thick hind legs equipped with black nuptial pads that enable them to grasp females during amplexus. Sexual dimorphism is also evident in the shape of the cloaca. The male's is hemispherical and the female's is cone-shaped and projects slightly.

Care: Eastern newts are fairly hardy in captivity and often readily available from captive-bred stock, rendering them a fine "first newt." The aquatic phase of the Eastern newt is perhaps the easiest to maintain at home. Depending upon their range, these animals can be a bit more tolerant of warmer temperatures than other salamanders.

An aquarium with an easily accessible land area is ideal. Because they are small animals, Eastern newts may be maintained in well-planted aquariums. The land area can be a gravel bank or merely some floating cork bark. Eastern newts need to come out of the water and rest but do not travel extensively or feed on land.

All food is taken in the water and their food preferences are quite wide. The aquatic adult stage will feed upon nonliving food; Reptomin food sticks and trout chow are good staples. They will also readily consume blackworms, mosquito larvae, tiny earthworms, brine shrimp, and small insects.

Individuals in the eft, or terrestrial, stage will take live food only. Efts may be fed 1/4-to-1/2-inch (6–13 mm) crickets, blackworms, tiny earthworms, and leaf litter invertebrates.

Although efts have a fairly thick skin and are more suited to a terrestrial existence than many salamanders, care must be taken that they do not dry out. Moist retreats and a shallow water bowl should always be available. Efts preparing to enter the aquatic phase will become dark in color; at this point the terrarium's water area should be increased.

Breeding: Amplexus may last for several hours and occurs in shallow, quiet ponds in spring or fall, depending upon the range. The female is grasped about the head and chest region from above and is released when the male deposits a spermatophore that the female then takes up into her cloaca. The 200 to 300 eggs are individually attached to water plants, generally in the spring.

Egg incubation lasts from three weeks to two months, again depending upon range. Breeding can be achieved in captivity mainly through temperature manipulation and a change in the light phase. Northern populations do best if given a winter cooling period of several months. They may be refrigerated to temperatures as low as 35°F (1.5°C) in shallow water or damp sphagnum moss. Those from the southern parts of the range would require only a temperature dip to about 50 to 59°F (10–15°C) and the period can be shortened to two weeks.

Adults will consume the eggs, so they are best removed after spawning occurs. Live plants

This striped newt is exhibiting paedomorphism; it is sexually mature, but retains external gills and will not take up a terrestrial existence.

A pair of Eastern newts, **Notophthalmus viridescens viridescens,** *in amplexus.*

form the best substrate for the eggs, although in the absence of these females will use sticks, stones, and plastic plants. The eggs should be kept with a very light aeration.

Larvae: Eastern newt larvae are less than .4 inches (1 cm) in length upon hatching. Newly hatched brine shrimp and finely chopped black-worms are the best starter foods. One can experiment with dried foods once the larvae begin to feed regularly.

Because of the size of the larvae, a bare-bottom tank is best so that the food is not lost between cracks in the gravel. Metamorphosis is dependent upon a variety of factors, including water chemistry, temperature, and the character of the surrounding habitat. Certain subspecies of the Eastern newt remain in the larval form throughout their life, exhibiting neoteny, but this is not the common lifestyle. Generally, the larvae transform into a land-dwelling form at about three months of age and a size of approximately 1.6 inches (4 cm).

In its unique red eft stage, the Eastern newt is entirely terrestrial.

Eft Stage

Eastern newts are fairly unique in their lifestyle, exhibiting three separate forms. The terrestrial stage is referred to as the eft stage. The eft is an animal that grows to slightly under 4 inches (9.6 cm), is bright orange or red in color, and has a thicker, more roughened skin

The adult aquatic phase of the broken-striped newt, **Notophthalmus viridescens dorsalis.**

than the aquatic form. This stage lasts from one to three years. During this time the animals live in moist areas, generally within a forested habitat. They are completely terrestrial, feeding upon small invertebrates among the leaf litter.

Their bright coloration is a warning of the powerful skin toxins that these animals possess. Adult newts in the aquatic life stage also contain skin toxins, although they are not clothed in the bright warning colors of the eft. At the

end of the eft stage, the animal returns to water and takes on the coloration of the adult aquatic phase, greenish brown with red dots or stripes. At this point they are sexually mature and ready to breed.

The eft stage is occasionally skipped. Most often this occurs among populations living along the eastern coastal plain of the United States and on Long Island in New York. So we can see that among these animals we have a field ripe for investigation to determine the causes of the variety of lifestyles present. Some populations seem to exhibit the different modes with no apparent rhyme or reason, although of course one is there.

Subspecies: A variety of subspecies are occasionally available. The central newt, *Notophthalmus viridescens louisianensis,* has only tiny red spots or may lack spots completely, and

The black-spotted newt, **Notophthalmus meridionalis,** *differs from its relatives in appearance and range.*

The terrestrial (eft) stage of the striped newt, **Notophthalmus perstriatus.**

ranges from eastern Texas to Lake Superior. It interbreeds with other subspecies of the Eastern newt, giving rise to animals with a variety of color patterns and background marking patterns. The eft or land stage is generally skipped, especially in the more southerly portions of the range. In the southeastern coastal plain, the central newt often exhibits neoteny, skipping the aquatic adult and the land stage.

The Peninsula newt, *Notophthalmus viridescens piaropicola,* is limited in range to peninsular Florida, and is found in quiet canals, ponds, and ditches. The Peninsula newt is much darker, generally, than the red-spotted newt and may appear almost black. The eft stage is rare and neoteny is common.

Along the coastal plain in North and South Carolina we find the broken-striped newt, *Notophthalmus viridescens dorsalis.* It has a red dorsal lateral stripe bordered with black and

An adult (terrestrial) broken striped newt.

broken in one or two places along the head and body. The eft stage is generally present, and the aquatic adults are found in quiet pools of water.

Related Species: The striped newt, *Notophthalmus perstriatus,* has a red lateral dorsal stripe that is continuous along the animal's body, breaking only near the head and tail. The striped newt ranges from southern Georgia to northern Florida.

The black-spotted newt (*Notophthalmus meridionalis*) has large black spots but lacks the red ones typical of related species. It occurs from south Texas into Mexico and is limited to the moist areas around ponds and swamps.

Japanese Fire-Bellied Newt (*Cynops pyrrhogaster*)

Range and Habitat: This newt exhibits a largely aquatic lifestyle and ranges in size from 3.6 to 5 inches (9–12 cm). It is a member of the family Salamandridae and is native to eastern China and Japan. The Japanese fire-bellied newt inhabits quiet bodies of water that support heavy plant growth.

Description: The upper surface of this newt is dark brown to jet black and sometimes slightly spotted with red, and the abdomen is strikingly patterned in orange or deep red. The bright coloration makes quite a contrast against the dark background and serves to warn potential predators of the powerful skin toxins. Obvious paratoid glands are located along the sides of the head. During the breeding season, males develop a threadlike extension of the tail tip and the cloaca enlarges.

Care: The Japanese fire-bellied newt makes a fairly hardy terrarium inhabitant. An aquarium for adults can be composed mainly of water with floating cork bark as a land area. They do not wander extensively on land or require land-based shelters, being content to float around on cork bark while they rest. Fire-bellied newts become rather tame in captivity, readily accepting food from one's fingers.

The thin tail extension and swollen cloaca of this Japanese fire-bellied newt, **Cynops pyrrhogaster,** *identifies it as a male in breeding condition.*

Japanese fire-bellied newts rely heavily upon scent to find their food and thus will accept Reptomin food sticks and trout chow. Other favorite food items are earthworms, black-worms, snails, tiny fishes, and insects. All food is taken in the water.

As they naturally inhabit still waters, filtration should be mild. Despite their aquatic nature, these newts can climb up the sides of glass, so the aquarium needs to be well covered. Japanese fire-bellied newts become fairly stressed at temperatures over 76°F (22°C) and are then subject to fungal infections and skin diseases.

Breeding: Japanese fire-bellied newts should be overwintered on wet moss at 40 to 50°F (5–10°C) if breeding is desired. Courtship begins in the water with the male butting the female's body with his head and blocking her progress should she try to move away. The paratoid glands are rubbed along her body, and the tail is used to fan pheromones designed to stimulate her into courtship behavior.

The spermatophore is picked up by the cloacal lips in typical salamander fashion. Eggs are individually attached to aquatic plants, with the tip of a leaf folded over each egg by the female. The incubation period is short, generally less than two weeks.

Larvae: The larvae sport external gills and develop into the semi-aquatic adult form within a few months. Sexual maturity is within two years.

Fire Salamander
(*Salamandra salamandra*)

Range and Habitat: This member of the family Salamandridae is a terrestrial species frequenting mossy woodlands and moist mountain habitats in southwest Asia and Europe, as well

The brilliant warning coloration of the Japanese fire-bellied newt.

as a small portion of northwestern Africa, a continent noted for its lack of salamanders. They leave their underground or decaying log retreats to forage on wet nights.

Description: The fire salamander, a brilliantly colored creature, is in great demand in the pet

This beautiful fire salamander, Salamandra salamandra, *exhibits an unusually large amount of yellow in its coloration.*

The subspecies **Salamandra salamandra gallaica** *in typical fire salamander habitat.*

trade. The dorsal surface is generally jet black mottled with bright orange or yellow. The subspecies *Salamandra salamandra fastuosa* is bright yellow with jet black lines going down the body, legs, and tail.

The brilliant colors are a warning to other creatures that the fire salamander is protected by virulent toxins. The paratoid glands are quite large and noticeable, and smaller glands are spread throughout the skin. When disturbed, this salamander secretes a visible, sticky poison, which, unlike that of other salamanders, can be projected outward for some distance. Fortunately, fire salamanders usually abandon this habit once accustomed to captivity.

Care: Fire salamanders make quite hardy terrarium inhabitants but are extremely sensitive to warm temperatures. Most become stressed at temperatures over 70°F (19°C), and death may result from sustained exposure to temperatures above their preferred range (60–65°F [14–16.5°C]). Individual fire salamanders have survived for more than 50 years in

The pores of the fire salamander's large paratoid (poison) glands are clearly visible in this photograph.

Interesting Fact

The common name of fire salamander is not given in recognition of bright coloration, but rather arose in Europe from the belief that these creatures were born of fire. The fire salamander is rarely encountered in the wild. Those fleeing logs tossed into fireplaces were thus believed to have arisen spontaneously.

captivity, which is quite an incredible record for an amphibian. They are stoutly built, and adults can be up to 12 inches (30.4 cm) long. An animal of that size and coloration is quite spectacular.

In captivity they exhibit many of the traits that have been described for the tiger salamander, *Ambystoma tigrinum*. Fire salamanders are very visually oriented and seem to anticipate regular feeding times, often leaving their retreats as one approaches the terrarium, apparently in anticipation of a meal. They will feed from the fingers or tongs and are not shy about moving about in broad daylight once they are acclimatized to captivity.

A woodland terrarium with a gravel bottom, a water reserve, and a variety of damp retreats is ideal, or they can be housed in a simple sweater box situation.

Fire salamanders are territorial by nature and will choose the same retreats for a long period of time. Therefore, when cleaning the tank, their shelters should be returned to their usual locations.

Fire salamanders' appetites are quite easy to satisfy in captivity. Earthworms, blackworms, slugs, waxworms, crickets, and other small invertebrates are all readily taken.

Fire salamanders have a tendency to become obese in captivity. This is not a healthy situation and may interfere with breeding. Adults can be fed three small meals per week or two slightly larger meals.

Breeding: Fire salamanders have a quite unique breeding strategy. They do not lay eggs, but rather give birth to live larvae. Individuals

Some **Salamandra salamandra giglioli** *are clad in brilliant orange.*

Some individual **Salamandra salamandra bernardezi** *exhibit little coloration; others are boldly marked.*

living at high elevations give birth to fully formed small salamanders, skipping the larval stage completely.

Depending upon their range, mating takes place in the spring or fall. The male's hold upon the female during the mating process is unique. He slides below her and grasps her from this position with his forelegs, holding her above himself for several hours. During this time he is

also stimulating her by rubbing the base of his tail on her cloaca and his head on the lower part of her chin. He deposits the spermatophore on land, and the female takes it into her cloaca.

The female remains on land within her normal territory until the following breeding season. She then migrates to the edge of a cool, highly oxygenated pool or stream and there deposits up to 70 larvae.

Larvae: The larvae are about 1 inch (2.4 cm) long, have external gills, and are mottled brown and tan with lighter patches at the bases of the limbs. Uniquely, fire salamander larvae are born with four limbs; other species are limbless when they hatch. Among populations that give birth on land, the young are fully formed miniatures of the adult, without external gills.

The larvae are ravenous and grow quite rapidly. They can be raised as has been discussed for other aquatic salamander larvae, and readily accept brine shrimp and chopped blackworms. One might experiment with dried foods also.

Terrestrial larvae and newly transformed salamanders will take chopped blackworms, sow bugs, tiny earthworms and waxworms, and 1/4-inch (6 mm) crickets.

Fire salamander larvae leave the water in two to three months at a size of 1 1/2 to 2 inches (3.8–5 cm). Animals raised at unnaturally high temperatures tend to transform early and at a small size.

Subspecies: Ten to eleven subspecies of fire salamander are currently recognized. *Salamandra salamandra terrestris* is found in Western Europe. There are four subspecies on the Iberian Peninsula, one in Corsica, one in North Africa, one in Italy, and two in Asia.

Emperor or Crocodile Newt (*Tylototriton verrucosus* and *T. shanjing*)

These colorful members of the family Salamandridae are also referred to as mandarin or the orange-striped newts. There is some discrepancy regarding the identity and ranges of the seven *Tylototriton* species that are currently recognized.

Range and Habitat: *T. verrucosus* is basically terrestrial, being found in moist forests in

The banded fire salamander, **Salamandra salamandra terrestris,** *is found in Western Europe.*

mountainous areas, occasionally at elevations up to 10,000 feet (3,000 m). It ranges from western Yunnan, China, to northern reaches of India, Myanmar, Nepal, Thailand, and Vietnam. It is believed to occur in Laos and Bhutan as well.

The brilliantly colored *T. shanjing,* usually sold under the name *emperor newt,* is restricted in distribution to western, central, and southern Yunnan, China.

Crocodile newts spend most of their time beneath rocks, logs, and decaying leaves. In the more arid portions of the range, they appear to be opportunistic breeders, reproducing in small pools whenever water is available. Outside of the breeding season, they are generally active during the wetter times of the year, with some populations spending the entire dry season in aestivation.

Crocodile newts are generally fairly inactive animals, and their food requirements are correspondingly smaller than would be indicated for a more active animal of similar size. Because of the harsh environments in which they live, these animals can be fairly hardy if kept properly. They are, however, species of high elevations, and even though some of the areas in which they occur get quite warm, they avoid the heat by burrowing or becoming dormant. In captivity, they do best at cool temperatures.

Description: Adults can reach over 7 inches (18 cm) in length and are stoutly built. They appear to be armored, because of bony ridges just below the skin and the thick, toxin-rich warts.

Care: Although individuals from certain populations appear to tolerate temperatures as high as 80°F (24°C), breeding behavior and growth is curtailed. They are most active at temperatures of 65–70°F (16.5–19°C), but this

Boney ridges below the skin lend the colorful emporer newt, Tylototriton verrucosus, *an armored appearance.*

may vary among animals originating from different parts of the range.

Adult mandarin or emperor newts will accept slugs, small snails, earthworms, blackworms, waxworms, sow bugs, and crickets as food. They seem to enter shallow water areas within the terrarium more often than do other terrestrial species and occasionally feed there.

Breeding: Breeding has occurred spontaneously in captivity, but a careful look at the climate of the habitat of origin would probably be required to breed this species regularly. A dry/wet cycle, or perhaps even a rain system, would likely be useful in stimulating reproduction.

Courtship attempts last, in some instances, for several days. The eggs are attached to floating objects, plants, or plant roots within two

A particularly brilliant California newt, **Taricha torosa.**

Roads that intersect the migration routes of the California newt are responsible for high mortalities during the breeding season, with more than 200 newts per night killed in some areas.

In certain areas in California, short stretches of road are closed throughout the newt's breeding season, and in other regions specially designed crossings funnel newts into tunnels dug under the roadways.

Captive California newts, especially those from the northern parts of the range, benefit from a winter dormancy period. If not cooled during the winter, it appears that some will not reenter the water in the spring and may refuse to feed at that time.

Description: The California newt is somberly colored above. Generally black to reddish brown, the ventral area is bright orange or bright yellowish in color. The lower eyelid may also be orange. It grows to 7.2 inches (18 cm) in length.

Care: California newts will consume nonliving food items such as Reptomin during the aquatic phase. When they emerge onto the land, however, they generally take only live food. At this time they can be fed blackworms, earthworms, waxworms, and small insects.

weeks of fertilization. The eggs are individually attached to various substrates with threads, and will be consumed by the adults if left in the same enclosure.

Larvae: The larvae are tiny, about 1/2 inch (1.3 cm) in length, and hatch within two to four weeks, depending upon temperature. Daphnia, chopped blackworms, and newly hatched brine shrimp should be offered. Metamorphosis usually occurs within three to five months, at which time the granular skin texture and bony ridges begin to become evident.

California Newt (*Taricha torosa*)

Range and Habitat: A staple in the pet trade and bred in great numbers, the California newt is becoming increasingly difficult to find in its natural habitat. One of the major threats to the continued survival of the California newt is habitat fragmentation and commercial development.

Deadly Toxins

All members of the genus *Taricha* produce virulent skin toxins. Those possessed by the rough-skinned newt may well be the salamander world's most powerful, with a single adult packing enough poison to kill 25,000 mice, or several people.

Studies of wild populations have shown that they are major predators upon amphibian eggs and tadpoles.

California newts need to be kept cool, although specimens from the more southern parts of the range are able to tolerate 80°F (24°C) for a couple of months, provided they have access to water. Some individuals can be kept in water year-round; however, to be safe they should be given a choice and their behavior should be carefully monitored.

Breeding: A male grasps the female from above with both legs and will swim off while carrying her if another male approaches. During courtship, the male rubs his chin along the female's head and his cloacal area along hers. After a period of time, which may be up to several hours, they will sink to the pond or aquar-ium bottom, where the male will crawl over the female and deposit a spermatophore in front of her. She will then take this up into the cloaca and internal fertilization will occur.

Clumps of about 30 eggs are attached to underwater structures and the 1/2-inch-long (1.1 cm) larvae hatch in about two months. Transformation to the adult stage is generally completed within three months. These animals are fairly long lived and do not attain sexual maturity until at least five years of age.

Other Species: The closely related rough-skinned newt, *Taricha granulosa*, ranges north to southern Alaska. The belly is yellow to orange and the lower eyelid is dark in contrast to the orange lower eyelid of the California newt. The red-bellied newt, *Taricha rivulries,* is found in northern California. This is a strikingly

The rough-skinned newt, **Taricha granulosa granulosa,** *is protected by the salamander world's most powerful toxins.*

Limited in range to Northern California, the red-bellied newt, **Taricha rivularis,** *is strikingly colored in red and black.*

colored animal, black above with a bright red belly. The lower eyelid is dark.

Crested Newt (*Triturus cristatus*)

Range and Habitat: The crested newt and its close relatives occur in ponds and streams from central Europe south to Israel and east to the Ob River and Caspian Sea.

Remember to use caution in handling the crested newt and all salamanders. Touching one's eye after handling a crested newt will result in an intense burning sensation that in some cases will necessitate medical attention.

Description: The crested newt reaches about 6.4 inches (16 cm) in length, and is grayish to black above and orange with round black spots below. A comb-like dorsal crest develops in the males during the breeding season, when they enter the water. In both sexes, the tail also becomes more paddle-like to facilitate swimming, but only the males develop the high, showy crest.

Ommatotriton vittatus ophryticus and some other subspecies develop an incredibly high crest that starts at the nose area and ends at the tail. Male *Triturus cristatus* may also develop a white line along the sides of the tail, and breeding females sport a white line down the back. These colors and the crest are lost after the breeding period, at which time the animals usually return to land.

If prevented from returning to land, crested newts may exhibit signs of stress, thrashing about wildly, but certain subspecies can be habituated to a more-or-less permanent aquatic existence.

Care: During the aquatic phase, crested newts will accept nonliving food. In common with many other newts, however, they will generally feed only on living animals once they take up terrestrial existence.

Depending upon their origin, crested newts will exhibit different temperature preferences, but they generally do best if temperatures are kept fairly cool.

Crested newts from some populations can be kept in water year-round. However, they should be provided a land area as well, and their behavior must be monitored carefully.

The aquatic phase of the crested newt, **Triturus cristatus.**

Breeding: It seems that a change in water depth may stimulate breeding outside of the normal cycle. Breeding males tend to fight and, although severe damage is rarely inflicted, less dominant animals may become stressed and cease feeding.

Courting males position themselves near females and appear to direct pheromones toward them with their tails. Females thus stimulated follow the males, push against their tails, and eventually pick up the spermatophore that the male has dropped. Several hundred eggs are laid, each being individually attached to an aquatic plant. The female uses her back legs to bend the leaf of the plant around the egg.

The larvae generally hatch within a month and transform into the adult phase during the same summer at a size of 2.4 inches (6 cm). Sexual maturity occurs in approximately two years, but varies among different populations.

Captive breeding requires a winter cooling at 36 to 46°F (2–8°C). Crested newts, especially the larvae, are particularly sensitive to water quality and quickly develop skin problems in suboptimal conditions.

A male banded newt, **Ommatotriton vittatus,** *showing the spectacular crests and brilliant colors that develop during the breeding season.*

Sirenidae

Lesser Siren (*Siren intermedia*)

Range: Three subspecies of the lesser siren range throughout the southern and central United States.

Description: The western form, *Siren intermedia nettingi,* is the largest, attaining a length of 26 inches (66 cm). The eastern forms are difficult to distinguish from the greater siren, *Siren lacertina;* however, the lesser siren has 31 to 33 costal grooves, whereas the greater siren has 36 to 39.

Sirens are totally aquatic and have an eel-like body covered with thick mucus. Adults retain external gills, lack rear legs, and have tiny, nearly useless front legs. Sirens are toothless, but the jaws have sharp cutting edges, rather like a turtle's jaw. Large specimens can bite painfully.

Despite the fact that sirens retain external gills, they also develop lungs, which come in handy in the shallow, warm waters that the southern forms inhabit. Sirens aestivate in those areas of their range where droughts occur, and can survive for at least four months while buried in the mud. Under these conditions, the lesser siren forms a protective case around itself, with a small opening by the mouth. This cocoon, composed of shed outer skin layers, is parchment-like in texture and enables the animal to retain body moisture.

Care: The waters in which sirens occur are generally still, so swift currents within the aquarium should be avoided. They are best kept in fairly shallow water, generally of a depth in which the siren can rise to the surface to get air without actually having to swim. They do not appear to be active swimmers in the mid-layers of the water but rather move along the bottom when searching for food. Constant swimming to the top of a deep aquarium might prove stressful to the animal; in deep water, dead branches and roots should be provided as "stairways" to the surface.

The aquatic dwarf siren, **Pseudobranchus striatus,** *makes a fascinating aquarium inhabitant.*

In well-oxygenated tanks, sirens appear to rely mainly on their gills for respiration.

The western race of the lesser siren remains active and feeding at temperatures of 68°F (20°C) and can tolerate warmer temperatures as well. Determining the origin of one's animals is essential if a proper temperature gradient is to be provided. Animals from the more northern and perhaps far western parts of the range might need a slight cooling period to stimulate reproduction.

Sirens feed readily on earthworms and black-worms, and particularly relish soft (recently molted) crayfish. They also accept live minnows, shiners, shrimp, insects, and snails.

Breeding: The details of siren reproduction are not well known, with only a single captive breeding of the lesser siren reported as of this writing. Males do not appear to produce a sper-matophore as do other salamanders that prac-tice internal fertilization. However, eggs are deposited singly or in small clumps. If fertiliza-tion were external, the male would need to fol-low the female for a long period of time and fertilize each egg as it was deposited. This behavior has not been observed among sirens or any of the well-studied amphibians.

Sirens, therefore, present a problem ripe for investigation. Research of this nature can be of significant value to the herpetological commu-nity, and can be carried out by competent non-professionals.

Larvae: Lesser siren larvae hatch in approxi-mately two months at .4 inches (1 cm) in length.

Other Species: The dwarf siren, *Pseudo-branchus striatus*, makes an interesting aquar-ium inhabitant. It is similar to the other sirens in general body form, but is much smaller, reaching a maximum size of only 8.5 inches (21 cm).

Dwarf sirens are dark brown with one to four light tan to yellow stripes along the back and two broader stripes along the sides. There are five subspecies, mainly differentiated by the pattern of striping.

Dwarf sirens differ from the larger species in having three fingers on each hand as opposed to four. Also, their fingers are tipped with tiny horny claws, the function of which is as yet unknown. There is only one open gill aperture on the side of the head as opposed to three in the lesser and greater siren.

Dwarf sirens are native to the southeastern United States, and are most abundant in Florida. One theory holds that the dwarf siren's numbers have been boosted by the introduction into the southeastern United States of the water hyacinth (*Eichhornia* sp.). This plant appears to provide such an agreeable habitat for the dwarf siren that it has been able to spread into areas where it was not originally found. An incredibly diverse population of invertebrates, amphibians, and small fish also inhabit tangled masses of water hyacinths, providing food for the dwarf sirens.

Captive Care: In captivity, dwarf sirens do best in well-planted aquariums provisioned with shallow water of approximately 68°F (20°C). Live water hyacinth, water lettuce, pothos, and Peace lilies provide an ideal habitat. As with all aquatic salamanders, careful attention should be paid to water quality, and water used in the aquarium should be free of chlorine and chloramine.

Amphiumidae

In the amphiumas, one finds creatures that appear far removed from salamanders in both appearance and behavior. The amphiumas are eel-like in appearance, darkly colored, and have a great deal of mucus on the skin. They have four tiny limbs that are evident only upon close examination, and that are, it seems, useless to the animal. Each limb has one to three toes, depending upon the species.

All three amphiuma species are entirely aquatic, although the two-toed and the three-toed amphiumas will occasionally leave the water on wet nights to travel to new areas, and at egg-laying time. The tiny eyes are covered with skin and lack lids. In feeding, they appear to use the sense of smell and also respond rapidly to touch. If the end of their body rubs against a food item, they will instantly dart back and grab it.

Upon hatching, the larvae have external gills, but lose them within two or three months. One pair of gill slits is evident on the adults, but respiration is via their lungs and skin. Amphiumas lay beadlike strings of eggs, up to 200 for large animals, in a muddy depression hollowed out by the female below a log, board, or other such cover. The nesting area itself may actually be out of the water, but the eggs are generally in the water that collects in the bottom of the nest site.

Fertilization is internal and the female guards the eggs until they hatch. It is not known if she stays with the eggs during the entire incubation period or leaves to feed on occasion. Incubation, at least in the two larger species, takes five months.

Three-Toed Amphiuma (*Amphiuma tridactylum*)

Range: This animal's range extends from western Alabama into Texas and north to southeastern Missouri and Kentucky. Mating occurs from December to June, with nests being observed from April through October. As with the other two amphiuma species, it spends the day buried in the mud or below a shelter, and emerges at night to search for food.

Care: Capable of reaching 41¾ inches (106 cm) in length, this massive salamander requires a large, well-filtered aquarium.

There is little that the three-toed amphiuma will pass up in the way of food, so it is fairly easy to supply a well-rounded diet. Whole fish, earthworms, blackworms, recently molted crayfish, tadpoles, insects, and pink mice (offered only on rare occasions) are all readily accepted.

Extreme care must be exercised when placing your hand into the aquarium for cleaning or feeding purposes. In very unsalamander-like fashion, amphiumas respond with lightning speed to water movement, striking out and latching on to whatever gets in their way. Their powerful jaws and sharp teeth can inflict painful wounds. It is a good idea to use tongs to make sure that all animals in the tank are feeding and that biting does not occur during the feeding process.

Although amphiumas often inhabit fairly acidic waters in the wild state, this should not be taken as an invitation to ignore water quality. Ammonia within the tank will kill these animals as quickly as any other salamander. Because of their large size and voracious eating habits, frequent water changes are required,

Beware of Amphiuma Bites

Although the majority of salamanders cannot inflict a painful bite, amphiumas have sharp teeth and lash out at most anything that comes within reach.

and any tank decorations must be heavy and securely fastened. Amphiumas are also escape artists, and in their nocturnal prowling will certainly push up against the screen top of an aquarium and escape if able. Although they can survive some drying, death from desiccation will eventually occur—and who knows what mayhem they might inflict on the hapless kitten or puppy that gets in their way while they are trying to make their escape!

Two-Toed Amphiuma (*Amphiuma means*)

Range: The two-toed amphiuma is found mainly within the U.S. coastal plain area, from southern Virginia to Florida and into eastern Louisiana. Eggs are laid in June and July in the northern part of the range, and from January through February in the south. This animal is as quick to bite as the three-toed, and has been observed feeding upon snakes and small turtles.

Description: Exceeded in size only by the Japanese and Chinese giant salamanders, the two-toed amphiuma measures up to 45 3/4 inches (116.2 cm) in length. It appears that the two-toed and three-toed amphiumas occasionally interbreed where their range overlaps, and some authorities consider them to be a single species. When properly maintained, they can live a rather long time; one two-toed amphiuma was kept for 27 years in captivity.

Breeding: The keeping of amphiumas is not all that difficult, but breeding in captivity is another matter. Because they change habitats for breeding, one must be able to move the

The two-toed amphiuma is the world's third-longest salamander; note the tiny limbs and pitted sensory organs.

animals or to change their setup to stimulate breeding. A temperature and light regimen should be established following the pattern of the area in which the animal lives.

At the appropriate time of the year, one might try dropping the water level and creating a muddy bank area with debris under which the animals can burrow. A children's wading pool or something a little larger would be ideal for this.

One-Toed Amphiuma (*Amphiuma pholeter*)

Description: The one-toed amphiuma is the smallest and least known of the three species within the genus. It reaches 13 inches (31 cm) in length, and its breeding habits have been little studied. Far more secretive than the others, it spends a good deal of its time burrowed in the mud, in a hole of its own making or that of some other animal.

Range: *Amphiuma pholeter* is limited in range to the Gulf Hammock and Panhandle regions of Florida and southeastern Georgia.

Proteidae

Mudpuppy (*Necturus maculosus*)

Range and Habitat: The mudpuppy ranges from southwestern Manitoba and southern Quebec to Georgia and Louisiana. Human introductions are responsible for disjunct populations in several large rivers in the northeastern areas of its range. The various subspecies occupy a wide variety of habitats, ranging from still, shallow swamps to deep, cold lakes and swiftly flowing rivers.

Description: The mudpuppy is one of our largest salamanders, commonly reaching 13 inches (33 cm) in length, with a record of 17 inches (40.8 cm). The body is flattened to facilitate the animal's living under stones and logs, and the slime covering is profuse. Mudpuppies vary in color from rust to reddish brown or gray, and are marked with blue-black dots and blotches. They are sturdily built, with a wide head, external gills, and tiny eyes. The legs, which are fairly small and suitable for crawling along the bottom, do not assist in swimming.

The size of the gills depends upon the animal's habitat. Those inhabiting quiet or stagnant waters generally have large gills to facilitate oxygen uptake, whereas individuals from fast-moving streams have smaller gills, as the oxygen content is generally higher in such waters. Mudpuppies also possess lungs and can rise to the surface to breathe.

The name *mudpuppy* or *waterdog* seems to have arisen from the mistaken belief that these animals bark and from the fact that the wide head appears somewhat doglike.

Populations of the northern mudpuppy have been classified into several subspecies. One, the Lake Winnebago mudpuppy, *Necturus maculosus stictus,* is very large and dark gray to almost black in color. They are native to northeastern Wisconsin and Michigan, and one individual was collected at a water depth of 90 feet (27 m).

Care: The mudpuppy consumes nearly any small creature that it can overpower. Many populations are said to live chiefly on crayfish, and nearly all are fond of these crustaceans. Soft (newly shed) crayfishes, or those with the claws removed, are preferable. Other favorites include earthworms, blackworms, small fish, snails, and tadpoles.

They are extremely sensitive to high light levels and will be very difficult to observe in a brightly lit aquarium; a night-viewing lamp, available at reptile supply outlets, will be of great value in this regard. Hiding places are essential, even for most well-habituated individuals, some of which may emerge during the day to feed.

Mudpuppies are best kept in very large, well-filtered aquariums. An undergravel filter, perhaps with an external filter as well, is the best choice for filtration. Although they can rise to the

The mudpuppy, Necturus maculosus maculosus, *shelters below rocks and logs by day.*

═══ T I P ═══

Water Quality

As is true for all large aquatic amphibians, the mudpuppy's waste products are fairly toxic when released from the body. Because mudpuppies are very sensitive to water quality, efficient filtration and regular water changes are essential.

surface for air, they do better in well-aerated tanks so that they can remain on the bottom, relying upon their gills for breathing. Mudpuppies do not seem comfortable leaving their shelters and swimming to the surface, especially in large aquariums. The northern races are generally found in cool water, and this should be provided in captivity as well.

Breeding: Captive breeding, although not common, has been accomplished. Mudpuppies become sexually mature at four to six years of age. The eggs are laid individually in a cavity below a rock or log and take anywhere from six to ten weeks to hatch. The female guards the eggs during the entire incubation period. Detailed observations on this behavior—for example whether or not she leaves to feed and how she reacts to threats—would be most interesting.

Larvae: Mudpuppy larvae are nearly 1 inch (2.5 cm) long upon hatching, and they can take chopped blackworms and earthworms right away. They are, however, highly cannibalistic and need to be separated or kept in very large tanks with a good deal of cover and a constant supply of food.

Other Species: The Gulf Coast waterdog, *Necturus beyeri*, reaches only 8.8 inches (22 cm) in length, and inhabits flowing waters in a restricted area extending from eastern Texas to central Louisiana. The dwarf waterdog, *Necturus punctatus*, matures at a length of 4$\frac{1}{2}$ to 6$\frac{1}{2}$ inches (11.4–16.5 cm), and is found on the coastal plain from southern Virginia to south-central Georgia. It sometimes inhabits quite sluggish water. The Neuse River waterdog, *Necturus lewisi*, is restricted to the Neuse and Tar rivers in North Carolina, and the Alabama waterdog, *Necturus alabamensis*, ranges from central Georgia through the Florida Panhandle. Both of these animals are fairly small as mudpuppies go, reaching only 8 to 9 inches (20.3–22.9 cm) in length.

The Olm (*Proteus anguineus*)

Range and Habitat: In natural circumstances, olms seem never to see daylight or appear above the ground at all. They are found only in underground lakes and streams in a small area extending from the eastern Alps in Austria through Trieste and into western Yugoslavia. The well-oxygenated waters they inhabit flow over and through limestone, and hence are fairly high in calcium content and hard.

Having evolved in such a unique habitat, olms are extremely sensitive to any changes in their wild or captive environment.

Young olms have never been found in the wild, and are believed to dwell deep within the natal cave systems. Most of what is known about them has been discovered by biologists working in laboratories under special conditions.

Description: This oddest of salamanders reaches 11.2 inches (28 cm) in length and is elongated in shape. It has tiny, degenerated eyes that are hidden beneath the skin and weakly developed legs. The hands have three fingers and the feet two toes, and the reddish gills are external. One subspecies, *P.a. parkelj*, has been identified. It is black, and apparently has well-developed eyes.

Care: Olms have poorly developed lungs and external gills. Even in oxygen-rich water, they appear to come to the surface regularly for air. They have been observed to leave the water, and even to feed on land.

Being creatures of complete darkness, olms are extremely sensitive to and disturbed by light, and in captivity they will become stressed and die if suddenly exposed to bright conditions. However, it seems that they can be gradually habituated to light and will actually darken in color and begin to act normally in its presence. When returned to darkness, their coloration fades.

Although they have experimentally endured higher temperatures, olms are adapted to and do best at 42.8 to 53.6°F (6–12°C). In the wild they appear to feed mainly on tiny cave-dwelling crustaceans.

Olms are protected by the laws of the countries in which they occur, and are not available to hobbyists in the United States. They have been kept in private collections in Europe for some time, however, where some individuals have lived in excess of 15 years and have reproduced regularly.

Breeding: Males in breeding condition stake out territories and attack interlopers. Injuries from the fights are often serious. Gravid females also establish a territory that they defend against all intruders. Captive males have been observed to guard eggs, and females sometimes move eggs about with their mouths, but the purpose of this is not yet known.

Stranger still is the olm's habit of occasionally giving birth to live young. The normal breeding strategy is as yet unknown, or perhaps the animals can somehow switch their mode of giving birth, depending upon what circumstances within their habitat dictate.

The eggs generally take about two months to hatch in the cool temperatures at which olms live, and sexual maturity is not reached for at least two years. Up to 75 eggs have been laid by a single female over a period of one month. The larvae hatch out at approximately .8 inches (2 cm) in length.

Cryptobranchidae

Hellbender
(*Cryptobranchus alleganiensis*)
Range and Habitat: The hellbender ranges from the Susquehanna River drainage in southeastern New York south to the headwaters of the Chesapeake Bay and west to southern Illinois and northeast Mississippi. There are disjunct populations in northern Alabama and Georgia and in central and southwestern Missouri. It possibly occurs in some locations in Kansas as well. Despite this large range, the hellbender is threatened with extinction in many areas.

Hellbenders are restricted to clean, cool, flowing rivers and streams that have rocky bottoms and are well stocked with large hiding places such as flat rocks and logs. Studies have shown that hellbender population densities are directly linked to the availability of suitable shelters. The rivers and streams in which they live generally have fast-moving water and are usually devoid of cover, except for large structures such as rocks, tree stumps, or fallen trees.

Having evolved in cool, chemically stable waters, hellbenders are quite sensitive and are among the first creatures affected by the introduction of pollutants into the ecosystem.

A hellbender, **Cryptobranchus alleganiensis alleganiensis,** *consuming its shed skin.*

Description: The hellbender is the American representative of the family Cryptobranchidae, which includes the 5-foot (152 cm) long Japanese giant salamander (*Andrias japonicas*) and the Chinese giant salamander (*Andrias davidianus*). The hellbender is a giant among American salamanders, nearly the longest and certainly the heaviest, with an average length of 11½ to 20 inches (29–51 cm), and a record length of 29⅛ inches (74 cm).

Hellbenders are interesting in appearance to say the least. They have been known to grab fishing lines, and people unfamiliar with them often cut the line rather than deal with their bizarre catch. The flattened head and body, which are quite wide, have fleshy folds of skin along their sides. The skin is thick and there are longitudinal furrows along the throat. The tiny lidless eyes, located on top of the head, are nearly invisible. It is probable that the hellbender cannot form very distinct images, but senses light and dark only.

Recent work has shown that the entire skin surface of the hellbender is light-sensitive, with the sensitivity being greater in the tail and lower body region. This arrangement serves to warn the creature when its tail and lower part of the body are exposed from its rock hideaway and therefore subject to predation.

Like many aquatic salamanders, hellbenders possess a lateral line organ system similar to that evolved by fishes. This helps the salamanders to sense water vibrations and to orient themselves toward or away from predators or food items. Even within the same river, the coloration of individual hellbenders varies a great

Telltale Sign

In poorly oxygenated waters, hellbenders will rock from side to side, in order to increase the water flow over their loose skins and obtain additional oxygen. This behavior is an important sign that immediate action needs to be taken to increase the aquarium's oxygen level (and, perhaps, to decrease the temperature).

deal. Most hellbenders are dull brown in color and mottled with darker spots, but gray, olive green, and even orange and reddish specimens are encountered.

Care: Hellbenders must be kept in well-oxygenated water; even though the lungs can be used for respiration, they would be extremely stressed by having to leave their hideaways to rise to the surface. Hellbenders are only truly at home in very spacious containers in which they can be completely hidden most of the time. Well-adjusted animals might venture out on occasion to feed, but they are generally fairly secretive in nature.

Hellbenders do best under dim lighting and at cool temperatures, with 60 to 65°F (14–16.5°C) being safe for most populations. They are best maintained in a large refrigerated aquarium equipped with a powerful filtration system; trout storage tanks are ideal. Filtration should be through activated carbon. Strict attention must be paid to hygiene, with frequent water changes being the rule.

Hellbenders are extremely sensitive to additives to the water, so care should be taken to remove chlorine and chloramine from their water. Captive breeding has occurred, but it is the exception rather than the rule. Once habituated, hellbenders can do quite well if their requirements are met; captive longevity has exceeded 30 years.

Studies of free-living hellbenders have revealed that crayfish are a staple in the diet, and captives certainly relish them. Aquatic insects are also taken, as are snails, fishes, earthworms, tadpoles, and blackworms.

The hellbender is one of the few salamanders that can inflict a painful bite. Although they do not warrant the fear that many people feel toward them, one should be careful in handling

hellbenders, as they resent this process violently. Also, hungry animals will snap at anything that moves past their shelter, so care should be taken when working in their aquarium.

The skin is extremely sensitive and easily damaged by nylon nets. Ushering the animals into a plastic bucket is a safer way of moving them when necessary.

Breeding: A careful study should be made of the natural habitat of captive specimens, so that lighting, day/night cycle, water-quality parameters, and temperature can be adjusted to induce breeding. A large enclosure is required, and the male should be given the opportunity to choose from several nest sites. A strong water flow might be necessary to stimulate the male to breed or to choose a site. Because the nest opening always faces downstream, a similar situation should be created in the aquarium.

Females introduced into the aquarium should be removed after egg-laying, as the male will then defend the eggs from them and anything else in the tank. In contrast to most other salamanders, hellbenders practice external fertilization. The male hollows out a nest in the river bottom, always under a protective rock or some other source of cover, and then herds passing gravid females into the nest. There is no amplexus. The male ejects sperm into the water over the eggs when they are released by the female. A male will often have the eggs of several females in his nest.

Larvae: Larvae hatch out at the relatively large size of 1.2 inches (3 cm) in about 10 to 12 weeks. They lose their external gills when approximately 4 inches (10 cm) long; being fairly slow-growing, it takes about three years to reach this stage. Sexual maturity is not attained until at least five years of age, and

The stunning Iranian newt,
Neurergus kaiseri.

possibly occurs much later than that among some populations.

Adult hellbenders retain larval characteristics such as certain aspects of dentition and the lack of eyelids. They develop lungs, but do not seem to often use them for respiration, as they are very rarely observed to surface for air either in the natural or captive situation.

Hellbenders are completely aquatic and virtually helpless on land. They do not actually swim much, but crawl along the bottom. Perhaps their flattened appearance is an adaptation for moving about along the bottom of the often swift-moving rivers that they inhabit.

The lungs appear to be involved in buoyancy control, and their appearance and development has caused a great deal of discussion and confusion. Adults retain gill slits where the gills were located on the larvae (the name *Cryptobranchus* means "hidden gills"). Early researchers assumed the openings were connected to internal gills and that respiration occurred in that manner. It now seems that most respiration is cutaneous, with the many loose folds of skin along the body and head increasing the area available for oxygen absorption.

Subspecies: One subspecies of hellbender has been described. The Ozark hellbender, *Cryptobranchus alleganiensis bishopi,* has larger, darker blotches on its back than does the hellbender, and the lower lips are heavily spotted with black in contrast to the lightly spotted or unspotted lips of the hellbender. This animal is confined to portions of the Black River and the north fork of the White River in southeastern Missouri and Arkansas.

Species New to the Pet Trade

A number of newts and salamanders that have long been difficult or impossible to obtain are now being regularly bred in captivity. Most surprising of these is Anderson's salamander, *Ambystoma andersoni.* Somewhat similar in appearance to the closely related Mexican axolotl (*A. mexicanum*), this highly endangered salamander is limited in distribution to a single lake in Mexico.

Hobbyists and zoos are also working with the Chinese black-spotted newt, *Pachytriton labiatum,* and its relatives (known collectively as "paddle-tailed newts") and with the gorgeous Iranian newt, *Neurergus kaiseri.*

Unfortunately, the care of these and the many other species that are currently entering the trade is beyond the scope of this book. However, I'll be happy to entertain questions at *http://blogs.thatpetplace.com/thatreptileblog* or *findiviglio@thatpetplace.com.*

APPENDIX

Diseases of Newts and Salamanders

Symptoms	Possible Causes	Diagnosis
General		
anorexia	behavioral foreign body infections, toxins	review husbandry gastric wash X-ray, endoscope
weight loss	mycobacterial infection fungal	X-ray, CBC cloacal culture, liver biopsy
lethargy, nonresponsive	environmental factors, nutrition	review husbandry, diet cultures
edema, ascites	viral, bacterial infection water quality parasites, organ failure	culture lymph, CBC chemistries, test water
Skin		
erosion/ulceration	bacterial, fungal, mycobacterial infection, parasites	culture, biopsy lesion, acid fast and Gram's stain of cutaneous swab
discoloration	chemical insult behavioral, chromomycosis algae, trematodes	cutaneous swab for cytology, check water
edema	tadpole edema virus water osmolarity changes bacterial infection renal failure	check water quality culture, necropsy histopathology
cottony material	fungal (*Saprolegnia*) infection	culture, cytology of cutaneous swab
nodular mass	mycobacterial infection parasitic granuloma bacterial abscess, neoplasia	needle aspirate, biopsy, acid fast stain, culture, cytology

*The endangered Santa Cruz long-toed salamander, **Ambystoma macrodactylum croceum**, is found only in southern Santa Cruz and northern Monterey counties, California.*

Symptoms	Possible Causes	Diagnosis
Musculoskeletal		
spindly legs	nutritional deficiency	no cure, provide balanced diet to adults
deformed/soft bones	calcium:phosphorus imbalance vitamin D deficiency UV light deficiency congenital defects	X-ray review diet, husbandry, replace UV bulbs
weakness	nutritional deficiency generalized infection	review diet, biopsy, necropsy
nodular masses	parasites, bacterial abscesses mycobacterial abscesses neoplasia	biopsy, culture, acid fast stains X-ray
fractures	trauma, nutritional deficiency	X-ray, review diet
Gastrointestinal		
regurgitation	parasites foreign bodies bacterial infections	gastric wash, cytology endoscopy, X-ray fecal exam for parasites
diarrhea	bacterial infection parasites toxic insult	cloacal culture, fecal exam for parasites check water quality

Adapted from "Amphibians" by Dr. Bonnie Raphael, *Exotic Pet Medicine*, 23(6):1271, 1993.

adaptation features of an animal that assist its survival in a particular environment. Adaptations may be genetic or behavioral.

aestivate to enter a state of reduced activity during hot, dry weather.

amplexus amphibian mating position (used by most frogs and many salamanders) during which the male clasps the female with one or two pairs of legs.

aquatic living mainly in the water.

arboreal living mainly in trees.

chemo sensation detection of particular chemicals in the environment.

cloaca common opening into which the reproductive and digestive tracts empty.

clutch total number of eggs laid during one breeding episode.

cold-blooded see *ectothermic.*

courtship behavioral displays and interactions that occur before and during the mating process.

cutaneous respiration transfer of oxygen and carbon dioxide through the skin.

ectothermic animals whose bodily temperature varies with that of the external environment. Formerly referred to as *cold-blooded.*

eft immature, land-dwelling stage in the life cycle of a newt.

environment all of the factors (thermal, chemical, psychological, etc.) that affect an animal.

external fertilization union of egg and sperm outside the body of the female.

gestation period of development of the offspring that occurs inside the body of the female.

gular pertaining to the throat.

habitat physical characteristics of the area in which an organism lives.

hybrid offspring derived from the mating of two animals of different species.

internal fertilization union of egg and sperm inside the body of the female.

Jacobsen's organ (vomeronasal organ) structure in some mammals, reptiles, and amphibians that allows for chemo sensation of particular molecules in the environment.

larvae early, immature form in the development of salamanders and certain other animals.

lateral line arrangement of sense organs in the skin of certain aquatic animals that allows for the detection of water-borne vibrations and, possibly, chemo sensation.

leucistic pertaining to the condition (caused by genetic mutation) in which normal pigments are absent. The animal is white, but may also have certain areas of normal coloration.

metamorphosis transformation, usually involving a change in appearance, from one stage of an animal's life to another.

neotenic retaining larval characteristics in sexually mature animals.

nuptial pads roughened areas that develop on the forearms of some male amphibians during the breeding season. The pads assist the male in grasping the female during amplexus.

olfactory pertaining to the sense of smell.

paedomorphic see *neotenic.*

paratoid gland protrusions on the skin of certain amphibians that contain toxins used to discourage, injure, or kill predators.

permeable characteristic of a surface that allows for the passage of certain substances.

pheromones chemical secretions that communicate messages to other animals—such as readiness to breed or claim to a territory.

population group of animals of the same species that occupy a particular area.

The highly endangered Anderson's salamander, **Ambystoma andersoni.**

race a taxonomic grouping below the sub-species level. Animals of the same race share certain characteristics that differentiate them from others of their species or subspecies.

range geographic area within which an organism is found.

sexual dimorphism physical characteristics that differentiate the sexes.

spermatophore packet containing sperm, which the female takes into her body.

substrate substance, such as wood, rock, or moss, on which an organism dwells.

subspecies distinct group of animals within a species, often inhabiting a range isolated from other members of the species.

terrestrial living chiefly on the land.

tubercle a projection from the skin of an animal. Burrowing salamanders frequently have tubercles on their feet to assist in digging.

vomeronasal see *Jacobsen's organ.*

Important Note

Nearly all salamanders produce noxious and potentially fatal skin toxins. When swallowed, newt toxins have caused cardiac arrest leading to human fatalities. Do not handle salamanders with open cuts on your hands, and always wash thoroughly after holding a salamander—toxins transferred to the eyes via the fingers have led to temporary blindness.

Salmonella and other microorganisms can be transmitted from animals to people. Some of these can be lethal, especially to young, elderly, or immune-compromised people. Aquariums and utensils used in animal care should never be cleaned in sinks used for food preparation. Consult your doctor about surface disinfection, hand-cleaning, and related concerns. For precautions about potential electrical hazards associated with terrarium keeping, see page 31.

INFORMATION

Internet Resources
That Reptile Blog
(blogs.thatpetplace.com/thatreptileblog)

In his role as animal husbandry consultant for ThatPetPlace.com (the world's largest pet store), Frank Indiviglio posts several new articles each week on the natural history, captive care, and conservation of salamanders and other amphibians and reptiles. Readers can also pose questions and share their observations with others.

www.caudata.org/

The longest-running amphibian enthusiast site on the Internet, *caudata.org* is an unparalleled resource for amateur salamander keepers and professional herpetologists.

www.frogforum.net/forum/

Although chiefly devoted to the care and natural history of frogs, there is a good deal of interest here for salamander enthusiasts.

www.research.amnh.org/herpetology/amphibia/index.php

www.amphibiaweb.org/

www.iucnredlist.org/amphibians

Veterinary Care
Arizona Exotic Animal Hospital
http://www.azeah.com/

The hospital's founder, Dr. Kevin Wright, is one of the world's foremost exotic animal veterinarians and coauthor of the classic *Amphibian Medicine and Captive Husbandry.* Dr. Wright has posted a variety of much-needed amphibian, fish, reptile, bird, and mammal care sheets on the hospital's website. Phone and e-mail consultations are available at *http://azeah.com/Services.asp?id=79.*

Live Animals and Supplies
ThatPetPlace.com
237 Centerville Road
Lancaster, PA 17603
www.thatpetplace.com
(717) 299-5691

ThatPetPlace.com carries a full line of terrariums, substrates, foods, misters, filters, lighting systems, health products, books, and everything else you'll need to keep and breed newts and salamanders, all of which can be shipped worldwide. Live specimens are available at the store as well.

Michael Shrom
E-mail: shrommj@ptd.net

This premier amphibian breeder supplies a wide array of healthy, captive-bred newts and salamanders, including a number of species that are not commonly available elsewhere.

Books and Articles
Behler, J. L. *The Audubon Society Field Guide to North American Reptiles and Amphibians.* New York: Knopf, 1979.

Conant, R., and J. T. Collins. *A Field Guide to Reptiles and Amphibians: Eastern and Central North America.* Boston: Houghton Mifflin Harcourt, 1998.

Duellman, W. E., and L. Trueb. *Biology of Amphibians.* New York: McGraw-Hill, 1994.

Halliday, Dr. T., and Dr. K. Adler. *The Encyclopedia of Reptiles and Amphibians.* New York: Facts on File, 1986.

Hoff, G. L., F. L. Frye and E. R. Jacobson (eds.). *Diseases of Amphibians and Reptiles.* New York: Plenum, 1984.

Indiviglio, F. *The Everything Aquarium Book.* Avon: Adams Media, 2003.

Murphy, J. B., K. Adler, and J. T. Collins. *Captive Management and Conservation of Amphibians and Reptiles.* Ithaca, NY: Society for the Study of Amphibians and Reptiles, 1994.

Petranka, J. W. *Salamanders of the United States and Canada.* New York: Harper Collins Publishers, 1998.

Raphael, Dr. B. L. "Amphibians," *Exotic Pet Medicine*, 23(6): 1271, 1993.

Stebbins, R. C., and R. T. Peterson. *A Field Guide to Western Reptiles and Amphibians.* Boston: Houghton Mifflin Harcourt, 2003.

Stebbins, R. C., and N. W. Cohen. *A Natural History of Amphibians.* Princeton, NJ: Princeton University Press, 1995.

Magazines and Journals

Copeia
www.asih.org

Herpetologica
www.hljournals.org/perlserv/?request=
get-archive&ct=1

Journal of Herpetology
www.ssarherps.org/

Reptiles Magazine
www.custmag.com/rep

Organizations
Frank Indiviglio
E-mail: fjindiviglio@aol.com
Consultant:
• Zoo, museum, aquarium, and private exhibit design
• Animal husbandry
• Book authorship and review
• Field research
• Acquisition of captive-bred amphibians, reptiles, invertebrates, and mammals

The Maritime Aquarium, Norwalk, CT
www.maritimeaquarium.org

The author helped to design several exhibit areas in this excellent aquarium, including one for salamanders and other amphibians.

The Staten Island Zoo, Staten Island, NY
www.statenislandzoo.org/

The world-famous Carl Kauffeld Hall of Reptiles, recently renovated with the author as consultant and graphics writer, features a wide array of amphibians and reptiles.

The Brooklyn Children's Museum, Brooklyn, NY
www.brooklynkids.org

This well-known museum is unique in exhibiting salamanders and frogs that survive in urban habitats. The author served as consultant for the 2008 renovation.

American Museum of Natural History, New York, NY
www.amnh.org

The Bronx Zoo, Bronx, NY
www.bronxzoo.com

I N D E X

Dedication

This book is dedicated to my grandfather, Frank Hill, and my uncle, Sam Apa. Through a combination of genetics, patience, and understanding, they started it all. In Haiden Grenier (pictured here), I've since found pure joy and hope of a type I'd not expected, and my writing benefited immensely. I am very grateful. Nature and life hold much interest for you, I am sure . . . may you find it all.

About the Author

Frank Indiviglio is the animal husbandry consultant for ThatPetPlace.com, the world's largest pet store. He has spent a lifetime working at the Staten Island and Bronx Zoos, where, although specializing in amphibian husbandry, he cared for animals ranging from ants to elephants. Field research on anacondas, Pacific giant salamanders, and other animals, featured on television and in *National Geographic Magazine*, have taken him throughout the United States and abroad. Frank has long sought to promote responsible animal keeping and conservation through television and radio appearances, teaching, and by working as an environmental attorney for various conservation organizations.

Acknowledgments

This book, and the experiences that gave rise to it, would not have been possible without the sacrifices and encouragement of my mother, Rita Indiviglio, and my sister, Susan Schilling. I was inspired throughout by the kind companionship of Yukari Ishikawa. My sincerest gratitude goes out to each of you.

I have long availed myself of the expertise of the staff at the Bronx Zoo, and am especially grateful to William Conway, James Doherty, John Behler, and Bonnie Raphael.

I would also like to acknowledge the help of my editors, Pat Hunter, for her invaluable suggestions, and Kristen Girardi, for her fine work and thoughtful efforts on my behalf. Special thanks are due Zig Leszczynski for his wonderful photographs and a lifetime of contributions to our field and Richard and Patricia Bartlett for so many brilliant photos and, most importantly, for graciously sharing so much of interest with me throughout the years.

See the "Important Note" on page 99 for safety information regarding the handling of newts and salamanders.

Cover Photos

All cover photos by Richard D. Bartlett.

Photo Credits

Richard D. Bartlett: pages 2–3, 5, 9 (top), 10, 11, 12, 14, 15, 18, 19, 22, 23, 25, 27, 29, 30, 34, 36, 38, 41, 42, 43, 45, 46, 47, 48, 49, 53, 55, 56, 58, 59, 60, 63, 64, 65 (top), 66 (bottom), 67, 68 (top and bottom), 69, 70, 72, 73 (top and bottom), 74 (top and bottom), 75 (top and bottom), 76, 77 (top), 78 (top and bottom), 79 (top and bottom), 80, 82, 83, 84, 86, 89, 90, 93, 95, 97, 99; Zig Leszczynski: pages 4, 7 (top and bottom), 13, 32, 33, 40, 52, 57, 61, 65 (bottom), 66 (top), 77 (bottom), 81; Aaron Norman: pages 9 (bottom), 54, 85 (top and bottom).

All inquiries should be addressed to:
Barron's Educational Series, Inc.
250 Wireless Boulevard
Hauppauge, NY 11788
www.barronseduc.com

ISBN-13: 978-0-7641-4243-7
ISBN-10: 0-7641-4243-7

Library of Congress Catalog Card No. 2009036666

Library of Congress Cataloging-in-Publication Data
Indiviglio, Frank.
    Newts and Salamanders : everything about selection, care, nutrition, disease, and behavior / Frank Indiviglio.
        p. cm.
    Includes index.
    ISBN-13: 978-0-7641-4243-7
    ISBN-10: 0-7641-4243-7
  1. Newts as pets. 2. Salamanders as pets.
I. Earle-Bridges, Michele. II. Title.
SF459.N48I53 2010
639.3'785—dc22   2009036666

Printed in China
9 8 7 6 5 4 3 2 1